Exploring Science 7

THIS BOOK NOW BELONGS TO NIA SHANIA PAREKH IN CLASS 7·9 IN MR O'NEILLS TUTOR.

Mark Levesley
Sandra Baggley
Julian Clarke
Steve Gray
Penny Johnson
Marc Pimbert

PEARSON
Longman

Edinburgh Gate
Harlow, Essex

Contents

Human organs

What are the main organs in a human?

Our bodies contain a lot of different **organs**. Each one has a very important **function** (job) to do.

 1 Write down the names of five organs in the body.

 The brain is the most important organ in the body. It controls the body and makes sure that it works properly. The human brain is divided into two halves and each half has a different responsibility. The right-hand side controls imagination, and artistic and musical talent. The left-hand side controls memory, speaking, reading, writing and mathematical ability.

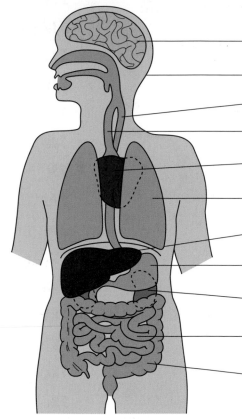

Brain: controls the body.

Skin: for protection and feeling.

foodpipe (gullet)

windpipe (trachea)

Heart: pumps blood.

Lungs: for breathing.

Liver: makes and destroys substances.

Stomach: stores and breaks up food.

Kidneys: clean the blood and make urine.

Small intestine: digests and absorbs food.

Large intestine: removes water from unwanted food.

Some organs in your body.

 2 Using the organs you chose in Question 1, copy and complete the following table.

Organ	Function

3 a) Which organ makes urine?   b) Which organ takes in air?
c) Name three organs that food passes through.

4 Write a report about the heart. You should include where it is and what it does. Find out what it is made of and how a doctor listens for it.

5 Find out more about another organ in the body which is not mentioned on this page.

You should know...

● **About all the organs on this page, where they are and what they do.**

What are the organs made from?

The photograph shows a human heart. You can see that it is made from different parts. The yellow part is fat and the brown part is muscle. These parts are known as **tissues**.

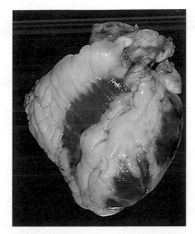

The heart contains muscle tissue and fat tissue.

 1 Name two tissues found in the heart.

The heart is an organ. It contains muscle tissue and fat tissue, as well as some other tissues such as nerve tissue. The heart has a very important function (job) to do. It pumps blood around the body to supply all of our cells with food and oxygen.

Plants have organs too.

 2 What is the function of the heart?

Stem: carries substances around the plant. It also holds the leaves in place.

Leaf: makes food by the process of photosynthesis.

Root: takes water out of the ground. It also holds the plant in the ground.

The photograph shows a root. You can see little hairs on it. This is **root hair tissue** which takes water out of the ground. Inside the root there is another tissue called **xylem tissue** (pronounced '*zy-lem*'). The xylem tissue carries water to the stem.

The root contains root hair and xylem tissues.

You should know...

- **Where the main plant organs are and what they do.**
- **That organs are made from tissues.**

 3 a) In which organ does photosynthesis take place?
b) Which organ contains root hair tissue?
c) Apart from the root, name a plant organ that contains xylem tissue.

 Plant leaves are organs that are designed to collect sunlight. The more area they can cover, the more sunlight they can collect. The biggest leaf ever found was from an Alocasia plant in Malaysia. It was 3 m long and nearly 2 m wide.

How do we use a microscope?

To get a closer look at what organs are made of, you need to use a microscope properly.

Microscopes make things appear much bigger than they actually are. They **magnify** things.

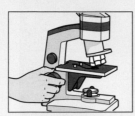

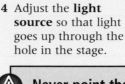

4 Adjust the **light source** so that light goes up through the hole in the stage.

⚠ **Never point the mirror directly at the Sun. This can permanently damage your eyesight.**

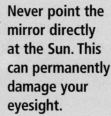

1 Place the smallest **objective lens** (the lowest **magnification**) over the hole in the stage.

2 Turn the **coarse focusing wheel** to make the gap between the **stage** and the objective lens as small as possible.

3 Place a **slide** under the clips on the **stage**. The slide contains what you want to look at (your **specimen**).

5 Look into the **eyepiece lens**.

6 Turn the coarse focusing wheel slowly until what you see is clear (**in focus**).

7 To see a bigger **image**, place the next largest objective lens over your specimen.

8 Use the **fine focusing wheel** to get your image in focus again. *Do not* use the coarse focusing wheel. You can break your slide and damage the microscope if you do. If you can't see anything, go back to a lower magnification.

1 A pupil sets up a microscope but can only see darkness when looking into the eyepiece lens. Write down what you think needs to be done to see the specimen.

2 Here is a set of five instructions on using the microscope. Write them in the correct order.
   A Look into the eyepiece lens.
   B Wind the coarse focusing wheel to focus.
   C Place the smallest objective lens over the hole in the stage.
   D Adjust the light source.
   E Place the slide under the clips on the stage.

3 Write down some rules of your own for:
   a) using a microscope safely   b) taking care of a microscope.

In 1590 a spectacles maker from Holland, called Zacharias Janssen, placed two lenses into a tube and invented the microscope.

You should know...

● **The main parts of a microscope and what they do.**

6

How can we prepare things to look at with a microscope?

A **specimen** is the object that you look at under the microscope. The specimen needs to be thin so that light can pass through it. To make sure that a specimen is as thin as possible we flatten it out by putting it between a **slide** and a **coverslip**. Coverslips also hold the specimen in place and stop it drying out.

The specimen in the top slide is too thick.

1 What is a specimen?

2 Why does a specimen need to be thin?

Onions are plant organs that grow underground. You are going to see what they are made of.

 Slides and coverslips are made of thin glass. Be very careful when you are using them.

When you have finished, write a report to explain how you prepared your slide, including:

- any problems you had
- what sort of stain you used and why
- a labelled drawing of one or two of your cells.

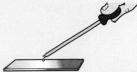

1 Take a slide and place a drop of water in the centre. The water may contain a **stain** to make the specimen show up better.

2 Using some forceps or your fingernails, peel off the inside layer of a piece of onion.

3 Place your onion skin onto the drop of water on your slide.

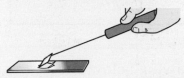

4 Using a mounted needle, lower a coverslip onto your onion skin. If you do this carefully and slowly you will not get any air bubbles.

When using a microscope, we need to know what **magnification** we are using. Both the eyepiece lens and the objective lens do some magnifying. How much they each magnify is often written on the side of the lens (e.g. ×10). The total magnification we get is given by:

magnification of the eyepiece lens × magnification of the objective lens

You should know...

- **How to prepare a microscope slide.**

3 Why do we use coverslips?

4 A microscope has a ×10 eyepiece lens and a ×15 objective lens. What is the total magnification?

What are the differences between plant and animal cells?

The first person to use a microscope to look at part of a plant was Robert Hooke. In about 1665 he looked at some cork and noticed what he thought looked like small rooms. He called them **cells**. There are animal cells and plant cells. These cells are far too small to see, so we need to use microscopes. Our bodies contain over 1 000 000 000 000 animal cells!

Robert Hooke (1635–1703).

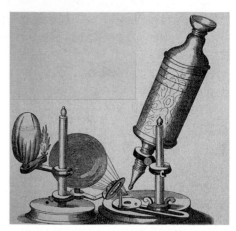

Hooke's microscope.

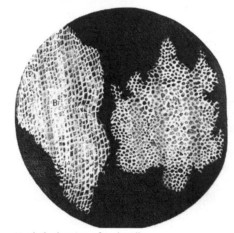

Hooke's drawing of cork cells.

1 a) Who first discovered cells?
   b) What did he use to see them?

2 a) Name five living things that are made from animal cells.
   b) Name five living things that are made from plant cells.

The drawing below shows the parts of an animal cell. The photograph next to it shows a real animal cell. It is taken from the inside of somebody's cheek.

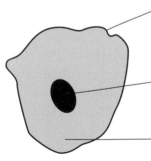

Cell surface membrane. This is like a very thin bag. It keeps the cell together and controls what goes into and out of the cell.

Nucleus. This is the 'control centre' of the cell. It tells that cell what to do.

Cytoplasm. This is a jelly-like substance. Many of the cell's activities take place here.

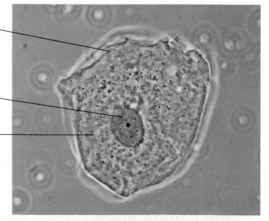

An animal cell (magnification ×2000).

3 a) What does the nucleus do?
   b) Name two functions of the cell surface membrane.
   c) What happens in the cytoplasm?

Plant cells look a little different from animal cells, but they also have cytoplasm, a nucleus, and a cell surface membrane. Plant cells have straighter edges and are more box-shaped. These cells are from a moss leaf.

Cell wall This is like a box with many large holes in it. It supports the cell and is very strong. It is made out of a substance called **cellulose**.

Vacuole This is a storage space filled with a liquid called **cell sap**.

cell surface membrane

nucleus

cytoplasm

Chloroplasts These are green discs that allow the plant to make food (by **photosynthesis**). They contain a chemical called **chlorophyll**.

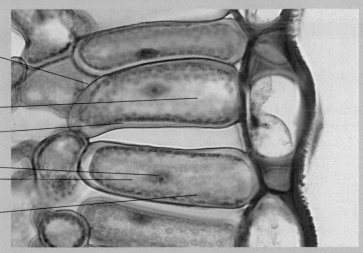

A plant cell (magnification ×1100).

 4 a) Write down the cell parts that both plant and animal cells have.
   b) Write down the cell parts that plant cells have but animal cells do not.

5 What makes plant cells green?

6 a) Draw a basic line diagram of a plant cell and label all of its parts.
   b) Make a table to explain what each part of the plant cell does.

 An average animal cell is about 0.02 mm across. An average plant cell is about 0.04 mm across.

Cell surface membranes are only 0.000 01 mm thick.

The animal cell in the photograph on the opposite page is 2000 times bigger than in real life. It has been magnified 2000 times. We say it has a magnification of ×2000.

 7 Measure the widest part of the animal cell on the previous page. Now work out its width in real life.

You should know...

● **Animal cells have a nucleus, cytoplasm and a cell membrane.**

● **Plant cells also have a cell wall, a vacuole and chloroplasts.**

● **What all of these parts do.**

Why do cells have different shapes?

Not all cells look the same. Some cells have a special shape to help them do a certain job.

Cells of the same type that are grouped together form a **tissue**. A tissue is a group of the same sort of cells, all working together to do a job. The group of muscle cells in the picture below is called **muscle tissue**.

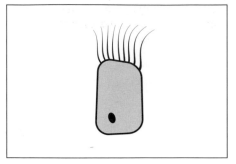

*A **ciliated epithelial** cell. The strands at the top (cilia) wave about to move things.*

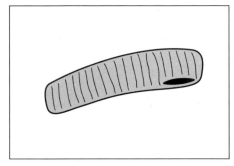

*–A **muscle cell** is able to change length.*

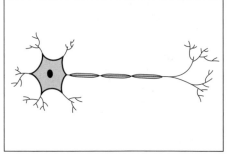

*A **nerve cell** (**neurone**) can be very long so that messages can be carried around the body quickly (at speeds up to 300 km/h).*

cilia

Ciliated epithelial tissue in a lung. The cilia wave together to move dirt out of the lungs. The cilia are killed off by cigarette smoke.

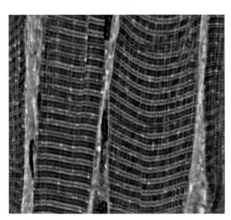

Muscle tissue allows us to move.

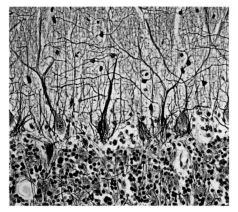

Nerve tissue in the brain.

1 What is a tissue?

2 Why are nerve cells so long?

3 What does muscle tissue allow us to do?

4 Where would you expect to find a lot of nerve tissue?

> An adult's body has over 200 types of cell. The longest are the nerve cells in the spine – these can be up to 1.3 m long. The smallest are another type of nerve cell found in the brain. These are only 0.005 mm long.

Not all the cells in a plant look the same.

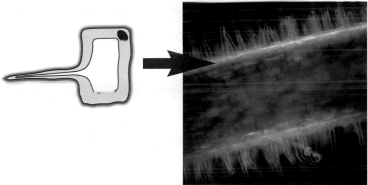

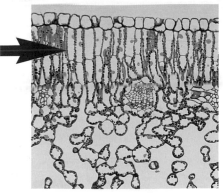

A **root hair cell** takes water out of the ground quickly. The root hair gives the water more surface area to get into the cell.

Root hair tissue (stained orange).

Palisade cells are packed with chloroplasts to help the plant make food.

Palisade tissue forms a layer near the top of leaves.

5 a) Which process, needing light, happens in palisade cells?
   b) Which part of the palisade cell does this process happen in?

6 a) What does a root hair cell do?
   b) How does the shape of a root hair cell help it to do this?
   c) Why are there no chloroplasts in a root hair cell?

Cells that have special shapes are said to be **adapted** to do certain jobs. The jobs that cells do, help us to live.

7 a) Explain how ciliated epithelial cells are adapted to remove dirt.
   b) What do you think happens to dirt in a smoker's lungs?

8 Make labelled drawings of a ciliated epithelial cell and a root hair cell.

9 Look at this picture of a xylem cell.
   a) How are xylem cells adapted to carry water?
   b) What do you think a group of these cells is called?

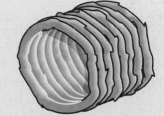

This is a xylem cell from a plant stem. Xylem cells join together to form hollow tubes, which carry water.

In 1839 Theodor Schwann (1810–1882) said that cells were the smallest living units from which all plants and animals were made. Before this time, people thought that tissues were the smallest parts. They also thought that tissues were not living.

You should know...

● Some cells are adapted to do special jobs.

● How ciliated epithelial cells, nerve cells and root hair cells are adapted.

● A group of the same sort of cells is called a tissue.

How do cells, tissues and organs work together?

Cells of the same type are grouped together to form tissues. Different types of tissues can be grouped together to make **organs**. Here are two examples.

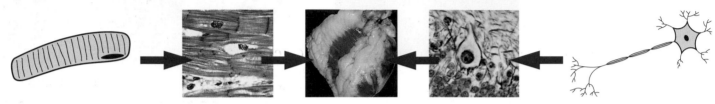

Muscle cells are grouped to form muscle tissue.

The heart contains muscle and nerve tissues.

Nerve cells are grouped to form nerve tissue.

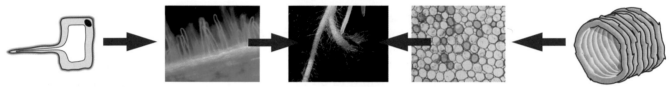

Root hair cells are grouped to form root hair tissue.

The root contains root hair and xylem tissues.

Xylem cells are grouped to form xylem tissue. The xylem tissue has been stained so that you can see where it is.

That's not the end of the story! Organs work together too. A set of organs working together is called an **organ system**. The heart is part of the **circulatory system**.

There are many other organ systems. Food is broken down in the **digestive system**. The brain is part of the **nervous system** which carries messages around our bodies. The lungs are part of the **breathing system**.

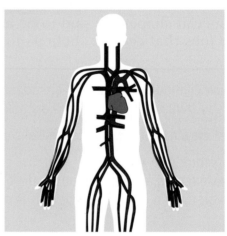

The **circulatory system** contains the heart and the blood vessels. It carries oxygen and food around the body.

1 Name two types of cells found in roots.

2 Name one sort of tissue that might be found in a plant stem.

3 Name another organ found in plants.

4 What is an organ system?

5 a) Name an organ in the circulatory system.
 b) What does the circulatory system do?

You should know...

● **Different tissues are grouped together to form organs.**

● **Different organs work together in organ systems.**

How are new cells made?

For something to be alive it must move, reproduce, sense things, grow, respire, get rid of waste (excrete), and need nutrition. These are the seven 'life processes'. Cells do all of these things and so help us to carry out the seven life processes. For example, our nerve cells help us to sense things.

All living things grow. For whole plants and animals to get bigger, they need to make more cells. The cells need to reproduce. They do this by dividing. One cell divides to make two new cells. This is called **cell division**.

1 Which life processes do the following cells help us with?
   a) nerve cells
   b) muscle cells

2 a) What is cell division?
   b) Which life process does cell division help with?

The nucleus of the cell splits into two.

A new cell membrane forms in the middle.

The new **daughter cells** get bigger.

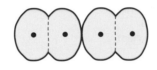

Once the daughter cells are full size, they too can divide.

When a cell divides, the two new cells are called **daughter cells**. The daughter cells made by cell division are quite small. Before they can divide they must grow to full size. To do this they require nutrition. Our cells get nutrition from the food we eat. That is why people who do not get enough food may not grow as tall as they should.

Sometimes cell division goes wrong and cells start to divide faster than they should. Cancer cells do this.

a cancer tumour

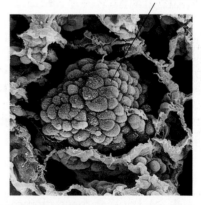

3 Look at this picture.
   a) Which cell is dividing (A, B or C)?
   b) How can you tell?
   c) Make a drawing of the dividing cell and label the parts.

4 Draw a diagram to show how cells divide.

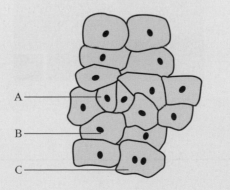

You should know...
● **Cells reproduce by dividing.**
● **Cells need nutrition to grow.**

What cells and organs do plants use for reproduction?

Although we often think of a flower as an organ, it is really an organ system. It is a collection of **reproductive organs** working together to make seeds. The seeds grow into new plants and this is how plants reproduce sexually.

Most plants have the male and female reproductive organs in the same flower. The reproductive organs make **sex cells**.

 1 a) Name the male reproductive organ of a plant.
b) List its parts.
c) A pollen grain is a cell. Which part of the cell controls it?

2 a) Name the female reproductive organ of a plant.
b) List its parts.
c) What is the female sex cell called?

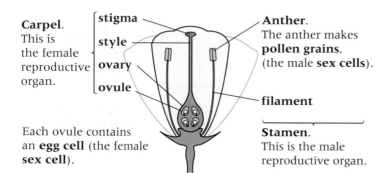

Carpel. This is the female reproductive organ.
stigma
style
ovary
ovule

Anther. The anther makes **pollen grains**, (the male **sex cells**).

filament

Each ovule contains an **egg cell** (the female **sex cell**).

Stamen. This is the male reproductive organ.

 Prospero Alpino (1553–1616) was the first person to realise that plants had male and female parts. He also introduced coffee and bananas to Europe.

Pollen grains need to be carried from the anther of one flower to the stigma of another. This is called **pollination**. The pollen grains are usually carried by insects or by the wind. Pollen grains carried by insects are large and have spikes on them so that they stick to the insects' bodies. Pollen grains that are carried by the wind are small and light.

 3 Suggest why pollen grains from wind-pollinated flowers are small and light.

4 a) Look at these pictures of the pollen grains. Which one is from an insect-pollinated flower? Explain your reasoning.
b) Work out how big these pollen grains are in real life.

A

Magnification ×200.

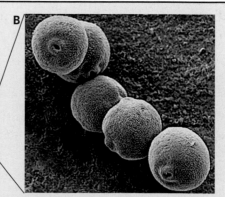

B

Magnification ×3000.

Once a pollen grain has landed on a stigma, a **pollen tube** begins to grow. The stigma makes a sugar solution to help the pollen tube grow down the style to the ovary. Eventually it reaches an ovule. The nucleus from the pollen grain goes down the tube and into the egg cell, found inside the ovule.

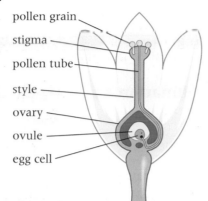

pollen grain
stigma
pollen tube
style
ovary
ovule
egg cell

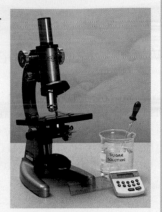

 What strength of sugar solution do pollen tubes grow best in?
- How would you look at the pollen tubes?
- How many different strengths of sugar solution would you use?
- What do you think would happen?

 5 How does the nucleus from a pollen grain get to the egg cell?

 Pollen from wind-pollinated plants causes some people to get hayfever. In the summer the number of pollen grains in the air can reach up to 3000 grains per cubic metre.

The pollen grain nucleus joins with the egg cell nucleus. This is called **fertilisation** and a **fertilised egg cell** is formed. The new nucleus inside the fertilised egg cell contains all the information needed to make a new plant. Half of this information has come from one plant and half from another plant. The new plant will have some features from both plants and so will be a new **variety**.

The fertilised egg cell grows and divides (makes copies of itself) and eventually an **embryo** is formed. The ovule becomes the seed with a hard outer seed coat. The ovary swells up and becomes the **fruit** around the seed.

6 Explain what is meant by 'fertilisation'.

7 What happens to a fertilised egg cell to turn it into an embryo?

8 a) Which feature of Plant C came from Plant A?
   b) Which feature of Plant C came from Plant B?

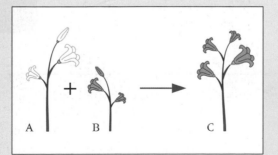

A   B   C

You should know…

- **Pollination is the transfer of pollen grains from one flower to another.**

- **Fertilisation is the joining of two nuclei from different sex cells.**

- **Fertilisation produces new plants which are different from the parent plants.**

What are cross-pollination and self-pollination?

Sexual reproduction should produce new varieties of plant. For this to happen, pollen from one flower needs to get to the stigma of another flower on a different plant. We call this **cross-pollination**. If pollen from a plant lands on a stigma from the same plant, then we call this **self-pollination**. Self-pollination will not produce new varieties of plant.

Plants use one of two ways to stop self-pollination happening. In most plants the anthers split open first. After they have released all their pollen, the anthers die and only then do the stigmas become mature and ready to receive pollen.

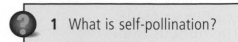

> **1** What is self-pollination?

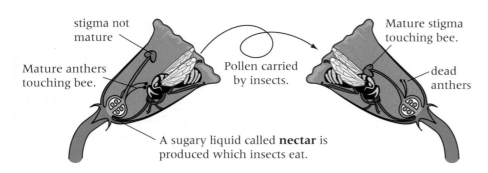

stigma not mature

Mature stigma touching bee.

Mature anthers touching bee.

Pollen carried by insects.

dead anthers

A sugary liquid called **nectar** is produced which insects eat.

Some plants use a different method to make sure cross-pollination happens. The plants have only male reproductive organs or female reproductive organs. For example, holly trees either have male flowers or female flowers, never both.

> **2** a) What is cross-pollination?
> b) Describe two ways of making sure that cross-pollination happens.

Only female holly trees wil produce berries.

Scientists often want to produce new varieties of plant. They take pollen from one plant and put it onto the stigmas of another plant. To stop self-pollination happening, all the anthers from the second plant are removed. Producing new varieties in this way is called **plant crossing**.

> **3** After putting pollen from one flower onto the flowers of another plant, scientists often wrap the flowers in clear plastic bags and wait for the seeds to grow.
> a) What part of a flower do they get the pollen from?
> b) What part of a flower do they put the pollen onto?
> c) Why do you think they use the plastic bags?

Which other animals can pollinate plants?

An animal that pollinates a plant is called a **pollinator**. Most pollinators are insects, which feed on nectar. Nectar is a sugary substance made inside the flower. The brightly coloured petals and the smell of the flowers helps to guide the insect to where the nectar is, so that pollen can be placed onto the insect or brushed off it.

Some flowers do not provide any nectar and attract insects in other ways. For example, Deadhorse Arum flowers give off the smell of rotting flesh and have flowers that, to flies, look like dead animals.

One of the biggest flowers in the world belongs to a tropical plant called the Titan Arum. Its flowers can grow up to 3 m tall and 1 m across. It gives off a smell like rotting fish, which attracts small bees.

Some orchids make themselves look and smell like female insects. The male insects try to mate with the flowers and get covered in pollen.

To this male wasp the flower looks and smells like a female wasp.

 Flowers that are pollinated by birds do not have a smell because most birds cannot smell.

Insects are not the only pollinators. Around the world, many birds, mammals and reptiles are used by plants to take pollen from one plant to another.

Even bats can be pollinators.

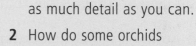

1 Why are flies attracted to Arum plants? Explain in as much detail as you can.

2 How do some orchids attract pollinators?

3 What might pollen stick to on a mammal pollinator?

4 Some flowers only open at night. What does this tell you about the pollinator?

How do animals reproduce sexually?

There would be no life on Earth if living things did not reproduce to make **offspring**. Most animals reproduce using **sexual reproduction**. This requires two **parents** – a male and a female.

Males make **sex cells** called **sperm cells** and females make sex cells called **egg cells**. One sperm cell joins (**fuses**) with one egg cell. Each sex cell contains a nucleus and these join in a process called **fertilisation**. This produces a **fertilised egg cell** which then grows into a new animal.

For fertilisation to happen, the sperm cells need to get to the egg cells. In some animals the male squirts sperm cells onto the egg cells as the female lays them. This is called **external fertilisation** and usually occurs in water.

In other animals, the male places the sperm cells inside the female. This is called **internal fertilisation**.

1 In animals, what are the male sex cells called?

2 How is a fertilised egg cell formed?

3 a) Name two animals that use external fertilisation.
   b) Name two animals that use internal fertilisation.

In external fertilisation some of the egg cells will not get fertilised because the sperm cells are washed away. The animals produce many egg cells to make sure that a lot get fertilised.

In animals which use internal fertilisation, fewer egg cells are produced. This is because the sperm cells are more likely to reach the egg cells.

4 In external fertilisation, not all the egg cells are fertilised. Why not?

Many animals which use external fertilisation do not look after the fertilised egg cells. As the fertilised egg cells grow into new animals, many of them are eaten by other animals. This is another reason for producing many egg cells.

Other animals protect their fertilised egg cells and offspring. Birds lay their fertilised eggs in nests and protect them. In some animals, like humans, the offspring grow inside the mother (in the **uterus**). The offspring are protected and can get all the things they need to grow from their mothers.

 Unlike most fish this mouthbrooder from Lake Malawi in Africa looks after its fertilised egg cells. After fertilisation, the female sucks them into her mouth where they grow into new baby fish.

? **5** What are the advantages of offspring growing inside the mother?

Human babies need care for a long time after they are born. They are not able to feed themselves or run about. Other newborn animals are more able to take care of themselves. A new-born giraffe can stand up and run after about twenty minutes. It takes about a year for a human baby to do this.

This new-born giraffe is only one hour old.

? **6** Why do you think it is an advantage for a baby giraffe to be able to get up and run soon after it is born?

7 The table shows the number of egg cells that different animals produce at a time.

Animal	Number of egg cells	Type of fertilisation
Bat	1	
Bullfrog	20 000	
Cat	4	
Cod	5 000 000	
Tiger	2	

a) How many egg cells does a bullfrog produce?
b) Write down two reasons why bullfrogs produce so many egg cells.
c) Copy and complete the table by writing the word 'internal' or 'external' in the last column.

8 Suggest a reason how the Lake Malawi mouthbrooder got its name. You may need to look up the word 'brood'.

You should know…

● **What internal and external fertilisation are.**

● **Human babies need much more care than other new-born animals.**

What do the parts of the human reproductive systems do?

The **reproductive organs** produce sex cells. They form an organ system called the **reproductive system**.

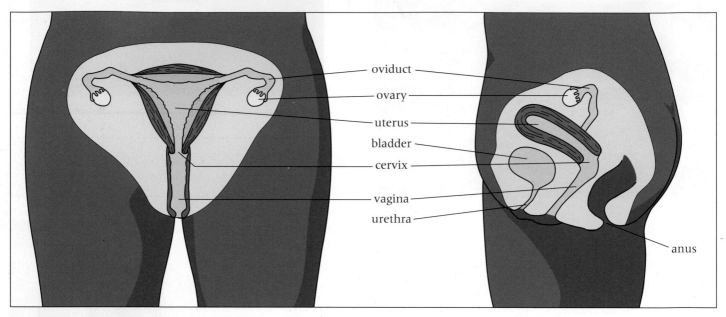

- oviduct
- ovary
- uterus
- bladder
- cervix
- vagina
- urethra
- anus

The female reproductive system.

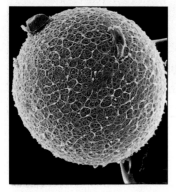

A human egg cell (magnification ×420).

In females, the ovaries contain hundreds of small, undeveloped egg cells. Once every 28–32 days, an egg cell from one of the **ovaries** becomes mature and is released into the **oviduct** (sometimes called the Fallopian tube or egg tube).

 1 a) What are the female sex cells called?
   b) Where are they released from?

The egg cells are **adapted** to carry out their **function** (job).

0.1 mm *smaller than a full stop*

The cytoplasm contains a store of food used to provide energy for the fertilised egg cell to develop.

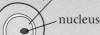

- nucleus
- The jelly coat helps to make sure that only one sperm can enter.

The oviduct is lined with small hairs (**cilia**) which move the egg cell slowly along the tube towards the **uterus**. The uterus is where the baby will develop. It has strong, muscular walls and a soft lining.

 2 How does an egg cell get to the uterus?

3 What is the cervix?

The lower end of the uterus is made of a ring of muscle called the **cervix**. The cervix holds the baby in place during pregnancy. The cervix opens into the **vagina**.

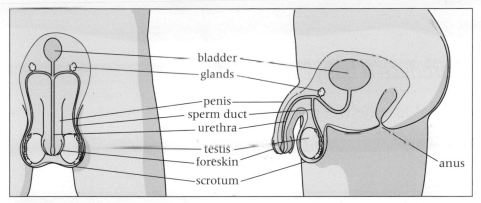

The male reproductive system.

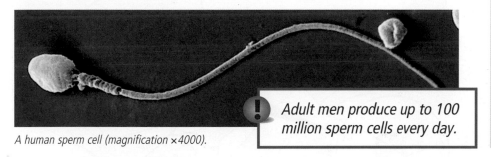

A human sperm cell (magnification ×4000).

 Adult men produce up to 100 million sperm cells every day.

Males make sperm cells in their **testes**. The testes are held outside the body in a bag of skin called the **scrotum**. Their position helps to keep the sperm cells at the right temperature to develop properly.

The sperm cells are adapted to carry out their function.

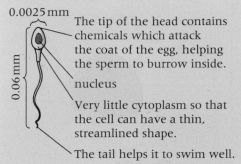

The tip of the head contains chemicals which attack the coat of the egg, helping the sperm to burrow inside.

nucleus

Very little cytoplasm so that the cell can have a thin, streamlined shape.

The tail helps it to swim well.

When sperm cells are released from the testes they travel up the **sperm ducts**, where special fluids are added from **glands**. The fluids help to give the sperm cells energy. Together the sperm cells and the fluids are called **semen**. The semen flows through a tube running down the centre of the penis called the **urethra**. The urethra also carries urine from the bladder, but never at the same time as semen.

The head of the penis is sensitive and is protected by a covering of skin (the **foreskin**). This is sometimes removed for religious reasons or because it is too tight. This is called **circumcision**.

After puberty, a man will produce sperm for the rest of his life. The ovaries in women stop releasing egg cells at about the age of 45–55. The time when this happens is called the **menopause**.

7 If a woman released an egg cell every 28 days for 35 years of her life, how many egg cells would she release in total? Show your working.

8 Which part of the sperm cell helps it to burrow into the egg?

9 Where does the developing fertilised egg cell get its energy from?

10 What is circumcision?

11 What is the menopause?

4 a) Where are sperm cells made?
  b) Do you think sperm cells like to be warmer or colder than the body?

5 What is semen?

6 What substances can the urethra carry?

You should know...

● **The parts and jobs of the male and female reproductive systems.**

● **How sperm and egg cells are adapted to their functions.**

● **Egg cells stop being released in females at the menopause.**

How does sexual intercourse produce a baby?

There are many forms of love. A special love between a man and a woman can lead to marriage. Men and women often show that they love each other by having sexual intercourse, also called 'having sex' or 'making love'.

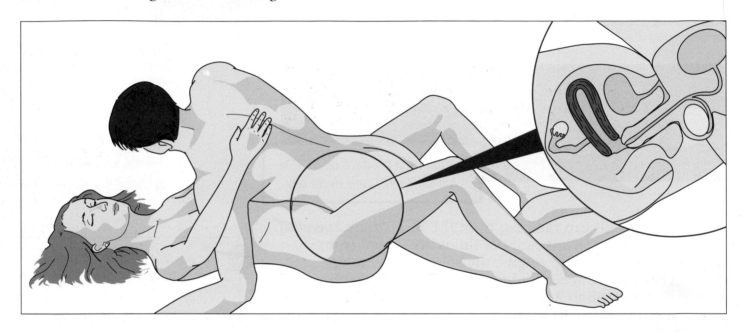

Before sex, the woman becomes excited and her vagina becomes moist. The man also becomes excited and his penis fills with blood. This makes the penis stiff and erect (an **erection**). The penis is inserted into the vagina and the man moves it backwards and forwards. Eventually semen is pumped out into the top of the vagina. This is called **ejaculation**.

 1 What fills the penis to make it stiff and erect?

2 What is ejaculation?

The semen is sucked up through the cervix. Small movements of the uterus wall carry it up to the oviducts. Here, the sperm cells start to swim up the oviducts. If a sperm cell meets an egg cell, the sperm burrows into it and **fertilises** it. In fertilisation, the nucleus of the sperm cell joins with the nucleus of the egg cell. Each nucleus contains half the instructions for a new human and so the baby will have features from both its mother and its father.

 3 What is fertilisation?

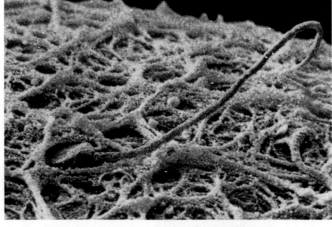

A sperm burrowing into an egg cell (magnification of ×4000).

The fertilised egg cell divides into two. Each of these cells then divides into two again. The cells carry on dividing and form a ball of cells, as they travel towards the uterus. In the uterus the ball of cells (called an **embryo**) sinks into the soft lining. This is called **implantation**. The woman is now **pregnant**.

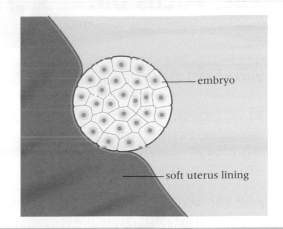

embryo

soft uterus lining

Twins

Sometimes, a woman might release two eggs at the same time. If both are fertilised, twins are produced. These twins will not be identical. Sometimes, though, when the fertilised egg cell divides in two, the two new cells get separated. Both of these cells now grow into an embryo and produce identical twins. Identical twins will either be two girls or two boys.

These twins are identical.

These twins are non-identical.

 Very occasionally, when the fertilised egg cell divides in two, the two new cells start to separate (as if they were going to produce identical twins) but do not separate fully. In this case the twins will be joined together, often at the hip. Joined twins like this are often called Siamese twins.

4 Where does fertilisation occur?

5 Only one sperm cell joins with the egg cell. What do you think happens to all the others?

6 What is implantation?

7 Explain why people get features from both of their parents.

8 a) How are non-identical twins produced?
   b) How are identical twins produced?

You should know...

● In sexual intercourse, the penis is inserted into the vagina.

● Fertilisation takes place when the nucleus of the sperm cell joins with the nucleus in the egg cell.

● This takes place in an oviduct and produces a fertilised egg cell.

● The fertilised egg cell divides into a ball of cells, called the embryo, which implants into the uterus lining.

What do people do if they can't have a baby naturally?

Most parents choose to start a family when the time is right for them. However, for some couples it is difficult to start a family. This is often due to a problem with the man's or woman's reproductive organs. Both the man and the woman may go to a hospital to have tests to find out what is wrong.

 1 Why do you think people like to choose when to start a family?

Damaged or narrow oviducts may stop sperm getting to the egg cells. In some cases, doctors can operate on the tubes to make them wider. If this does not work, the woman may be given a **sex hormone** to make her produce many egg cells all at once. These can be collected and added to the man's sperm cells in a special dish. The fertilised cells are then placed into the uterus lining, where they grow and develop.

Some men produce very few sperm cells (they have a low **sperm count**). In this case, one sperm cell is taken and injected into an egg cell using a very fine needle. Again, the fertilised egg is placed into the uterus lining.

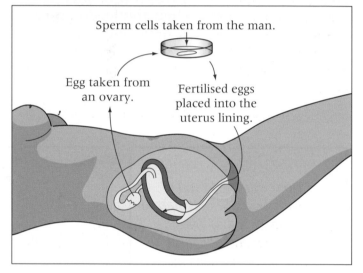

Sperm cells taken from the man.

Egg taken from an ovary.

Fertilised eggs placed into the uterus lining.

These methods of helping couples have a baby are called **IVF** ('*in vitro* fertilisation'). Babies born to couples who have used IVF are often called **test-tube babies**.

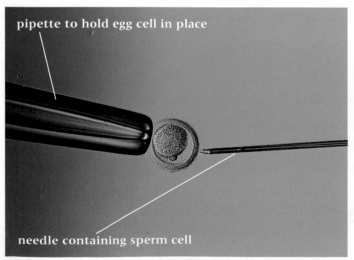

pipette to hold egg cell in place

needle containing sperm cell

 2 a) What does IVF stand for?
b) Why do some couples use IVF to help them have a baby?
c) Try to find out what the words 'in vitro' mean. (*Hint*: it's Latin.)

 The world's first 'test-tube baby', Louise Brown, was born in Oldham in 1978.

What happens during the menstrual cycle?

The **menstrual cycle**, lasting 28–32 days, is a series of events that occur in the female reproductive system. It is controlled by chemicals called **sex hormones**. These are made in the brain and ovaries.

In **menstruation** the soft lining of the uterus breaks apart. It passes out of the vagina along with a little blood. Another term used for menstruation is 'having a period'. A 'period' usually lasts for 3–7 days.

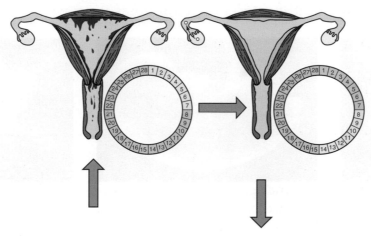

About 14 days after ovulation, if the egg has not been fertilised by a sperm cell, the lining of the uterus breaks apart again. The cycle starts again with another 'period'. If the woman becomes pregnant, the cycle stops.

Immediately after menstruation, an egg cell starts to **mature** in one of the ovaries. While this happens, the soft lining of the uterus starts to build up. About 14 days after the cycle has started, the egg cell is released. This is **ovulation**.

The egg cell is swept along the oviduct towards the uterus. If the egg cell meets a sperm cell it will be **fertilised**. The soft lining of the uterus is able to feed a fertilised egg cell. The lining is replaced each cycle to make sure it can do this. It continues to thicken for about a week after ovulation.

'Periods' usually occur once every 28–32 days, but this can vary quite a lot, especially when periods first start. Sanitary towels or tampons are used to absorb the blood.

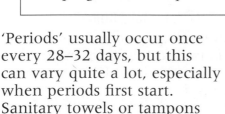

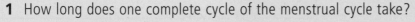

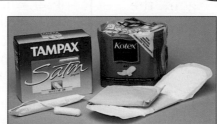

1 How long does one complete cycle of the menstrual cycle take?

2 a) What happens during menstruation (a 'period')?
   b) How long does menstruation last?

3 What happens about 14 days after menstruation starts?

4 Why does the soft uterus lining have to become thick?

5 How might a woman tell that she is pregnant?

You should know...

● The menstrual cycle lasts about 28 days. It begins with menstruation.

● Ovulation (release of an egg cell) occurs in the middle of the cycle.

Being pregnant

How does the fetus develop during pregnancy?

After fertilisation, the fertilised egg cell divides to form a ball of cells (an **embryo**). This **implants** into the soft lining of the uterus. The embryo gets food and oxygen from the blood in the soft uterus lining, to help it grow and develop. As it grows it becomes surrounded by a bag (the **amnion**) filled with a watery liquid (the **amniotic fluid**). The amniotic fluid protects the embryo as it grows.

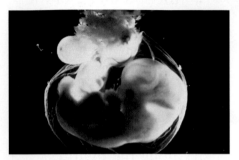 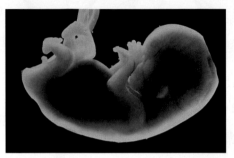 

*At five weeks the **embryo** is about 5 mm long. It has a small heart to pump blood.*

*After about ten weeks it has a full set of organs. It is about 4 cm long and is now called a **fetus**.*

After about fifteen weeks the fetus is 16 cm long. The mother can now feel its movements inside her.

The heart of the **fetus** (pronounced '*fee-tus*') pumps blood around its body and the **placenta**. The placenta is shaped like a plate and is attached to the uterus lining. At the placenta, the fetus' blood gets food, water and oxygen from the mother's blood. Waste materials (like carbon dioxide) are given to the mother's blood. The **umbilical cord** carries blood between the fetus and the placenta.

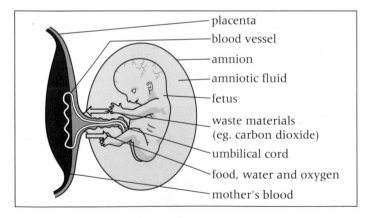

placenta
blood vessel
amnion
amniotic fluid
fetus
waste materials (eg. carbon dioxide)
umbilical cord
food, water and oxygen
mother's blood

The mother's blood does not mix with the fetus' blood. This is because the mother's blood is pumped around her body under a lot of pressure, which would damage the delicate fetus.

1 What protects the developing embryo?

2 After how many weeks can the mother feel the baby move?

3 What is the job of:
   a) the placenta
   b) the umbilical cord?

4 a) What does the fetus take from the mother's blood?
   b) What does the fetus give to the mother's blood?

5 The lungs do not work in a fetus. Why do you think this is?

6 Why does the fetus' blood not mix with the mother's?

You should know...
● **How the developing fetus is protected and cared for in the uterus.**

A healthy fetus

How can a mother care for the developing fetus?

During pregnancy, many changes happen in a woman's body. Her heart will beat faster, she will become heavier and she will need more food for energy each day. It is important that the mother has a healthy diet during pregnancy. She must provide the fetus with food, vitamins and minerals.

At an **ante-natal class**, mothers can do special exercises to strengthen their muscles.

 1 What changes will occur in a woman during pregnancy?

It is also important that the mother takes exercise to keep her muscles strong. She will need strong muscles during the birth.

Some viruses, alcohol, drugs and dangerous chemicals from cigarette smoke will all go through the placenta and into the fetus, where they can cause damage.

Viruses are tiny microbes which can cause diseases. The virus that causes rubella can cause the fetus to become deformed. Girls should make sure that they are vaccinated against rubella.

Too much alcohol will damage a fetus' brain (it can even cause severe brain damage). Illegal drugs, like heroin, also cause brain damage in the fetus.

 Sadly, sometimes drugs that are given to women to help them in pregnancy damage the fetus. In the 1950s a drug called thalidomide was taken by many pregnant women. It caused many babies to be born with very short arms and legs.

Doctors are very careful about which medicines they give to pregnant women.

 2 Why is exercise important during pregnancy?

3 a) What is a premature baby?
   b) Give one reason why this happens.

4 Which things should a mother avoid during pregnancy? Explain your answer.

 The blood of women who smoke carries less oxygen than it should, which means that the fetus may not get enough oxygen. A baby that has not received enough oxygen is likely to be born small and early (a **premature baby**).

You should know...

● During pregnancy a woman must eat a good diet and avoid harmful things like smoking.

What happens during and just after birth?

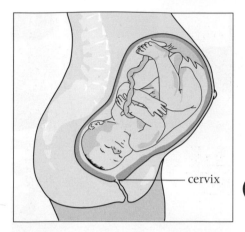

cervix

Pregnancy lasts about 9 months (40 weeks). This length of time is known as the **gestation period**. When the baby is due to be born the uterus starts to push or **contract**. This is the start of **labour**. Labour ends when the baby is born. The contractions are gentle at first but become more powerful as labour moves on. The muscles of the cervix then start to relax. The cervix gets wider to allow the baby through. At some stage, the amnion breaks and the amniotic fluid rushes out of the vagina.

1 What are contractions?

2 Explain what happens to the cervix during labour.

Once the cervix is about 10 cm wide, the strong contractions of the uterus push the baby through it. Usually the head comes out first and the baby starts to breathe almost immediately. The umbilical cord is then tied and cut. The scar left by the umbilical cord becomes the **navel** or 'belly button'.

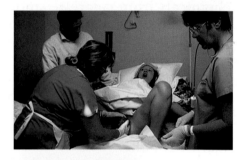

About half an hour after the birth, the placenta breaks away from the uterus and passes out through the vagina. This is called the **afterbirth**.

In the first few months, the baby needs to be fed on milk. The breasts contain **mammary glands** that produce milk. This milk contains nutrients to give the baby energy and help it grow. It also contains substances called **antibodies** which help to protect it from diseases caused by microbes. After a few months the baby can start to eat semi-solid food.

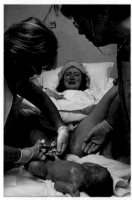

3 Copy and complete these sentences:
Pregnancy lasts for _____ months. When the baby is ready to be born, the uterus starts to _____ .
The baby is normally born _____ first. After being born the _____ _____ is cut. This leaves a scar called the _____ .

4 Explain what is meant by the 'afterbirth'.

5 How does a young baby get its food? Explain in as much detail as you can.

You should know...
- **Pregnancy lasts for 9 months.**
- **Contractions in the uterus push the baby out through the cervix and vagina.**

Growing up

What happens during puberty and adolescence?

Between the ages of ten and fifteen, physical changes start to happen in our bodies. These changes continue until the age of about eighteen. The time when these physical changes happen is called **puberty**. Girls usually start puberty before boys.

Puberty is controlled by chemicals called **sex hormones** that are released in our bodies. In girls, puberty starts when the **ovaries** start to produce sex hormones. In boys, puberty starts when the **testes** start to produce a sex hormone.

Emotional changes also occur, as well as physical changes. The time when all these emotional and physical changes occur is called **adolescence**.

Sex hormones make boys and girls become more interested in each other. The hormones may also cause mood swings.

Sex hormones can also be responsible for causing spots (**acne**).

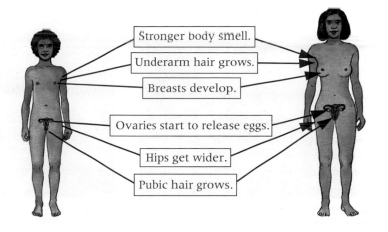

Stronger body smell.
Underarm hair grows.
Breasts develop.
Ovaries start to release eggs.
Hips get wider.
Pubic hair grows.

In medieval times, choirboys sometimes had their testes cut off (castration) before they reached puberty. This prevented their voices 'breaking'.

> **1 a)** What is puberty?
> **b)** What chemicals control puberty?
> **c)** Where are these chemicals produced in girls and boys?

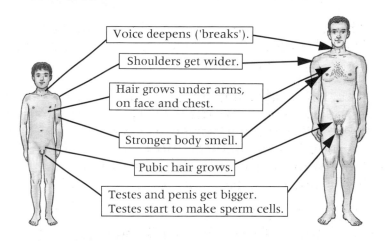

Voice deepens ('breaks').
Shoulders get wider.
Hair grows under arms, on face and chest.
Stronger body smell.
Pubic hair grows.
Testes and penis get bigger. Testes start to make sperm cells.

2 What is adolescence?

3 Make a list of the physical changes that happen to both boys and girls.

4 What do we mean by 'emotional changes'?

5 a) What is acne?
b) Imagine you work on an advice column in a magazine. Somebody writes to you saying that they have terrible acne. What advice would you give them?

You should know...
- **Puberty describes the time when physical changes happen.**
- **Both physical and emotional changes occur during adolescence.**
- **The changes start between the ages of ten and fifteen and end at about eighteen.**

What is in a habitat?

The place where an organism lives is called a **habitat**.

Woodland habitat.

Pond habitat.

meerkat

Desert habitat.

Arctic habitat.

Underground habitat.

1 Write down the names of two organisms that you would expect to find in each of the habitats shown in the pictures.

The word **environment** is used to describe the conditions in a habitat. Most of the conditions are caused by **physical environmental factors**. Examples include how much light there is, how wet it is, how much wind there is and how hot it is.

2 Describe the environment around you at the moment.

3 Describe the environment in each of the habitats on this page.

4 Find out what pieces of equipment you would need to measure the different environmental factors mentioned on this page.

A **quadrat** is used to take **samples** of an area. The quadrat is thrown a number of times and the numbers of the different species of plants inside it are counted. An environmental factor, such as the amount of light falling on the area inside the quadrat can also be measured. Using this technique you can see if there is a link between the environmental factor and the plants living there.

Using a quadrat.

P How would you investigate why different numbers of one plant grow in different areas of a habitat?
- How would you measure the environmental factor?
- How would you sample the area?

Organisms have features to help them live in their habitats. They are **adapted** to live there. Fish have gills and fins. These are **adaptations** for living in water. Their fins will not let them walk on land and their gills will not let them breathe air. Fish are *not* adapted to living on land.

5 How are ducks adapted to:
a) swim on water
b) fly?

All the animals and plants that live in a habitat make up a **community**. Members of communities may share adaptations to cope with the problems of living in a particular habitat. For example, many small animals and plants which live in fast flowing rivers are adapted to stop them being swept away.

Some animals and plants only live in certain small areas of a habitat. Centipedes live in woodland. They can be found under logs but not at the top of a tree. Smaller areas where things live are called **microhabitats**. All the places where a type of organism can be found are called its **distribution**.

 Even your body is a habitat! Head lice live in a microhabitat – human hair! They suck blood from people's scalps.

 6 Look at the list below. Which of these things are physical environmental factors?

light   frog   wind   bush   ant   fungus   temperature   bird

7 The picture shows a common frog.
a) Name the frog's habitat.
b) Write down an adaptation that helps the frog to live in its habitat.
c) Frogs have thin skins that need to be kept damp. Why is a frog not adapted to living in a desert?
d) Find out why the frog has a thin skin.

You should know...

● The place where an organism lives is a habitat.

● Organisms are adapted to living in a certain habitat.

● An environment is the conditions in a habitat. Physical environmental factors cause these conditions.

● Small places in a habitat where certain things live are called microhabitats.

● The distribution of an organism tells you where you can find it in a habitat.

Adept adaptations

How are animals and plants adapted to where they live?

Different organisms have different features which allow them to live in different areas. Their features make the organisms **adapted** to their **habitats**.

Good, colour vision to spot animals that might eat it.

Grey-brown colour does not show up well against tree trunks.

Long, bushy tail for balance.

Sharp claws for gripping tree trunks.

Long hind legs for leaping.

Grey squirrels are adapted to living in woodland.

2 How are squirrels adapted for:
a) climbing up tree trunks
b) balancing on branches
c) avoiding being eaten?

3 Why do duckweed plants want to get a lot of sunlight?

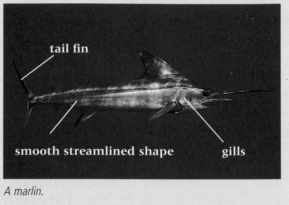

1 Three adaptations of a fish are shown in the photograph. What does the fish use each adaptation for?

tail fin

smooth streamlined shape   gills

A marlin.

Duckweed floats so that the leaves get plenty of sunlight for photosynthesis.

Duckweed is adapted to living in ponds.

How would you find out whether pond weed plants are only adapted to live in fresh water, or whether they can live in salty water too?
● What strengths of salt water solution would you use? (There are 30 g of salt in every litre of sea water.)
● What would you look for in the pond weed plants?

Black vultures live in the desert. They urinate on their legs to keep cool! The urine evaporates, which cools them down.

No leaves, which means that the cactus loses less water than a plant with leaves.

spines

Stem stores water.

Roots cover a large area to absorb as much water as possible when it rains. This saguaro cactus can absorb a tonne of water a day, after a storm.

A cactus is adapted to living in the desert.

Does not drink and gets all its water from its food.

Large ears allow heat to escape and for good hearing.

Large hind legs to run away quickly (at up to 70 km/h) from animals that might eat it.

A jack rabbit is adapted to living in the desert.

4 a) A cactus has spines on its stem. Why do you think these are useful?
b) Most cactus plants grow very slowly. Suggest why this is.

Small ears to stop it losing too much heat.

White fur so that it is not easily spotted.

Thick fur to help keep it warm.

Large hind legs to help it run away from animals that might eat it.

Big feet to stop it sinking into the snow.

Arctic hares are adapted to living in the Arctic.

Excellent senses of smell and vibration to detect animals to eat.

Streamlined shape to help it move through tunnels.

Large front claws to scrape earth to build tunnels.

Moles are adapted to living in an underground habitat.

5 a) A mole has very poor eyesight. Suggest why moles don't need good eyesight.
b) How do moles find their food?
c) Suggest one animal that a mole might eat.

6 The photograph shows a common rabbit.
a) What can you say about the length of common rabbits' ears compared with the other rabbit and hare on these pages?
b) Suggest why common rabbits have ears this size.
c) Which of the habitats on page 30 do common rabbits live in?
d) How do you think the fur colour of a common rabbit helps it to survive?

You should know...

● **Some examples of how plants and animals are adapted to their habitats.**

How do changes in their environments affect organisms?

The conditions in a habitat change from day to day. These are known as **daily changes**.

 1 How does the amount of light in a woodland habitat change during 24 hours?

Animals and plants adapt to these daily changes. Daisy flowers open during the day to attract insects for pollination. They close at night for protection. Some plants have flowers that open at night. The animals that pollinate these only come out at night. Such animals are **nocturnal**.

This cactus opens its flowers at night. The moth that pollinates it is nocturnal.

Some animals, like dormice, are nocturnal so that they are less likely to be seen and eaten. However, other animals, like owls, are also nocturnal so that they can catch and eat other nocturnal animals! Owls have excellent hearing which allows them to hear where mice are, even if they cannot see them.

 Mallow plant leaves turn to follow the Sun during the day. At night they turn back to face east, ready for sunrise.

Animals living along the sea shore adapt to the tides. Each day the tide comes in and goes out. Sea anemones have tentacles to feed underwater. When the tide goes out, they pull in their tentacles to stop them drying out.

 2 Draw two pictures of a daisy flower, one in the day and one at night.

A sea anemone under water.

A sea anemone when the tide is out.

P How would you find out if water fleas are found in different places during the day and at night?

There are also changes throughout the year. These are **seasonal changes**. In winter, some trees lose their leaves since there is not much light for photosynthesis. These are **deciduous** trees. **Evergreen** trees have tougher leaves and keep them all year round. Evergreen trees often grow quite far north where the summers are short. By keeping their leaves, they can start photosynthesising and growing again as soon as the conditions are right. Some plants, like poppies, die completely in the winter. Their seeds grow into new plants in the spring.

Animals are also adapted to survive winter. In the autumn, squirrels collect nuts and store them to eat during the winter. Many animals, like rabbits, grow longer fur to help keep them warm. The ptarmigan has brown feathers in summer and white ones in winter. It also grows feathers on its feet in the winter which act like snow shoes.

 3 Copy and complete these sentences.

A _____ tree loses its leaves in winter.
An _____ tree keeps its leaves in winter.

 4 Why do you think the ptarmigan's feathers change colour?

 An Arctic tern flies about 40 000 km each year as it migrates.

Some animals eat a lot in the autumn and then sleep through the winter. This is called **hibernation**. Hedgehogs hibernate in piles of leaves. Dormice, frogs and ladybirds also hibernate.

Birds sometimes fly away during the winter and go to warmer places where there is more food. This is called **migration**. When it is winter in the UK swallows migrate to South Africa where it is summer.

5 Why do animals which hibernate eat a lot in the autumn?

6 Write down how each of these physical environmental factors changes from summer to winter:
a) light   b) temperature   c) rain.

7 Write down how each of these organisms is adapted to survive winter:
a) hedgehog   b) oak tree   c) swallow   d) poppy.

8 Find out where the Arctic tern lives in the summer and where it flies to for the winter.

You should know...

● **Organisms are adapted to the daily and seasonal changes in their habitats.**

● **Deciduous trees lose their leaves in winter and evergreen trees keep their leaves.**

● **Nocturnal animals are adapted for activity at night.**

● **Animals which hibernate sleep through the winter and those which migrate travel to a warmer place.**

How are animals and plants adapted for feeding?

Predators are animals that hunt other animals. The animals that they hunt are their **prey**. Predators have adaptations that allow them to catch their prey. The predators in the pictures are from large open grassland (savanna) in Africa.

1 a) What is a predator?
  b) Name one predator from the African savanna.
  c) Name one predator that you might find in the school grounds.

Forward-facing eyes to spot prey.

Hooked beak acts like a pair of scissors to cut flesh.

Huge, sharp claws (talons) to grab hold of prey.

A Lanner falcon.

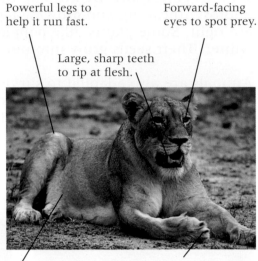

Powerful legs to help it run fast.

Forward-facing eyes to spot prey.

Large, sharp teeth to rip at flesh.

Sandy-coloured fur helps to camouflage it.

Sharp claws to grab prey.

A lion.

Animals that are prey have adaptations to help them avoid being eaten.

2 a) Make a list of adaptations that predators have in common.
  b) Make a list of adaptations that prey have in common.

Large ears to listen for danger.

Large horns for protection.

Eyes on the side of its head so that it can see behind.

Sandy-coloured hair for camouflage.

Long legs help it to be tall to see danger.

An oryx.

Large ears to hear danger.

Sandy-coloured fur for camouflage.

Eyes on the side of its head so that it can see behind.

Powerful hind legs to help it run fast.

A scrub hare.

Animals that eat other animals are called **carnivores**. They use senses like sight, smell and hearing to find their prey. Animals that eat plants are called **herbivores**. They use senses like sight and smell to find plants to eat.

3 Humans have senses. Which senses do we use to find food?

Woodlice are **decomposers**. They eat rotting wood and leaves. How would you investigate whether or not they have ways of finding their food?
- Think about the conditions in which rotting wood and leaves are found.
- You could use a **choice chamber**. The compartments can be filled with different substances.
- Calcium chloride removes moisture from the air.

anhydrous
calcium chloride
water

Many animals also have special adaptations for eating. For example, birds have different shaped beaks depending on what they eat.

Oyster catchers have long beaks to search in sand for shellfish.

Ducks have flat beaks to sift out weed and small snails from water.

Swallows have short, pointed beaks to catch insects in the air.

Finches have thick, strong beaks to crush seeds.

4 How is a Lanner falcon's beak adapted for what it eats?

5 a) What is a herbivore?
b) List all the herbivores on these two pages.

6 a) What is a carnivore?
b) List all the carnivores on these two pages.

7 Look back at page 34.
a) What is a nocturnal animal?
b) Name one predator that is nocturnal.
c) What sense does this animal use to hunt?
d) What is this animal's prey?

8 a) Many shellfish are found deep in the sand along beaches. Shelducks are ducks that live along the sea shore. Explain why shelducks don't eat shellfish buried in sand.
b) Suggest what shelducks eat.

9 Find out how a spiny anteater is adapted for what it eats.

You should know...
- **How some animals are adapted to finding food and feeding.**

How else can animals feed?

Most carnivores catch and kill their prey. Some are **scavengers** which means that they eat animals that have died or animals which have been killed by other animals.

Some other animals, called **parasites**, live on or inside other living animals and most feed on blood. The animals that they are in or on are called **hosts**.

Leeches are parasites which stick to animals using strong suckers. Medicinal leeches bite through the skin using three sets of jaws. They inject anaesthetic into the skin so that the host doesn't feel the bite. They also inject chemicals that stop the blood from clotting. The leeches normally drop off when they are full and they may not need to eat again for six months. Ticks (like those found on sheep), lice and fleas are also parasites that suck blood.

Some parasites live inside animals. Trypanosomes are microbes that swim in blood and absorb digested food from it.

Some types of worm, like tape worms, can live in an animal's intestines. They attach themselves to the wall of the intestine and absorb digested food.

Plants can also be parasites. Dodder is a plant with bright red stems. It attaches to and feeds off gorse and heather plants.

Vultures are scavengers. This buffalo has been killed by a lion.

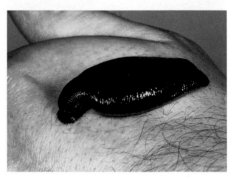

A medicinal leech.

Dodder on a gorse bush.

1 What is a scavenger?

2 Name a host of:
 a) ticks
 b) fleas.

3 Young medicinal leeches feed on thin-skinned frogs and not mammals. Suggest why this is.

4 The dodder plant has no leaves. Suggest why not.

5 Most parasites do not kill their hosts. Suggest why not.

6 Find out what disease trypanosomes cause in humans and how these parasites get into the bloodstream.

What are food chains and food webs?

A **food chain** is a way of showing what eats what in a habitat. Every organism contains a store of **chemical energy**. Animals eat things to get this store of chemical energy. The food chain shows that oryx eat grass and lions eat oryx. The arrows show that chemical energy is passed from the grass to the oryx and then from the oryx to the lion.

A plant starts off most food chains. Plants are **producers** because they make or produce their own food. Animals are **consumers**; they have to eat other things. A food chain always starts with a producer – even if it is dead! Some animals feed on dead leaves.

Animals that eat plants are **herbivores**. Animals that eat other animals are called **carnivores** or **predators**. A **food chain** is used to show what eats what. A food chain ends with a **top predator**.

On the African savanna it is not only oryx that eat grass. Many other organisms do too. To show this we need to use a **food web**. A food web can also show **omnivores** – animals that eat both plants and other animals.

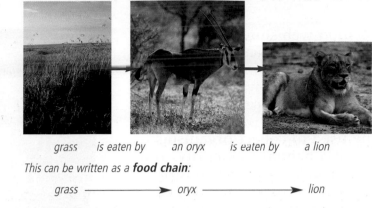

grass   is eaten by   an oryx   is eaten by   a lion

This can be written as a **food chain**:

grass ⟶ oryx ⟶ lion

 1 Look at the food chain above and name:
a) two consumers   b) a predator
c) a producer   d) a top predator.

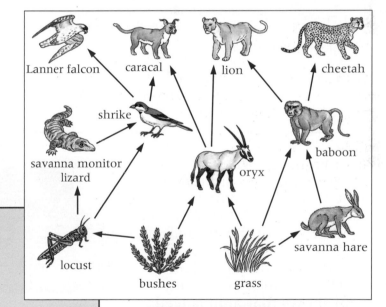

 2 Look at the food web.
a) What eats grass?
b) What do caracals eat?
c) Write down one of the two longest food chains in the food web.
d) Write a list of the organisms in this food chain. Describe what each is by writing one or more of these words next to it:

carnivore consumer herbivore omnivore producer top predator

e) Which of the words in part d) describes a baboon?

3 Why are plants called producers?

You should know...

- **How to understand food chains and food webs.**

- **The meanings of the words producer, consumer, herbivore, omnivore, carnivore, and top predator.**

How can we tell what eats what?

A food web shows what eats what in a particular habitat. There are a number of ways of finding out what organisms there are in a certain habitat. **Pooters** and **sweepnets** can be used to collect organisms from a habitat to identify. You can also hit the branches of trees with sticks and collect any organisms that fall off. This is called **tree beating**.

Using a pooter.

1 a) Where would you use a sweepnet?
  b) You would not use a sweepnet to collect animals from dead leaves. Why not?
  c) What would you use to collect animals from dead leaves?

2 If you remove any animals from a habitat to look at, you should always replace them where they were found. Why?

Using a sweepnet.

By finding out what organisms live in a certain habitat, you can start to make a food web for the habitat. Where the animals are found may give you an idea of what they eat. For example, aphids on a plant stem shows that aphids feed on that plant. Ladybirds may be found near the aphids.

aphids

3 Look at the photographs.
  a) The aphids in the photograph are feeding on a rose stem. What do you think the ladybirds are eating?
  b) What do woodlice like to feed on?
  c) What will eat the fly?

You can also find evidence for what an animal has eaten by looking at its waste.

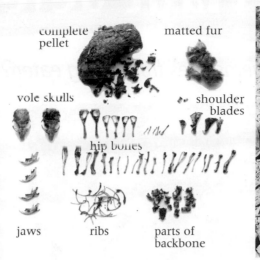

complete pellet   matted fur

vole skulls   shoulder blades

hip bones

jaws   ribs   parts of backbone

Thrushes are small birds that drop snails on stones to break their shells. The stones are called thrush anvils.

Owls swallow their food whole and then cough up the bits that cannot be digested. The coughed up bits come out as a pellet.

This dropping contains the seeds of what the bird has eaten.

Animal droppings are distinctive shapes. Identifying the animal droppings found near a damaged plant or dead animal will provide evidence to show what has eaten it.

Other evidence includes footprints or distinctive teeth marks. Snails leave trails of slime behind, which can often be seen around damaged plants.

Organisms **compete** with one another. Animals compete for food and space in a habitat. Plants compete for light, water and nutrients (mineral salts).

An expert will know that this hyena has been killed by a lion because of what the teeth marks look like.

4 Name one animal that an owl eats.

5 a) What do thrushes eat?
   b) How would you find evidence to support this?

6 Name two ways of finding out what a bird eats.

7 Birds eat the red berries on holly trees.
   a) Why do you think the berries are red?
   b) What does the holly tree do to stop animals eating its leaves?

8 Teeth marks are often found on the bark of trees. Suggest how you would go about finding out what animal made the marks.

You should know...

● **The ways in which we can find evidence of what eats what.**

● **That organisms in a habitat may compete with each other.**

How do plants protect themselves from being eaten?

Animals have many ways to try to stop themselves from being eaten. Plants also try to stop herbivores eating them. Living stone plants from southern Africa use camouflage.

Living stone plants from southern Africa use camouflage.

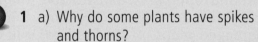

African acacia trees use thorns and poison.

Commonly, plants protect themselves with spikes and thorns. These can hurt the tongues of animals that try to feed on them and can puncture the skins of caterpillars. However, spikes and thorns do not always work. Most animals are put off by the thorns on an African acacia (*ack-ay-sha*) tree, but giraffes have very nimble tongues that can avoid the thorns. They also have thick, leathery mouths.

Although giraffes may feed on an African acacia tree, they are not able to feed on it for long. Soon after the giraffe has arrived the tree produces a poison which makes the plant inedible. The tree also releases a gas called ethene. Acacia trees nearby detect the ethene in the air and respond by producing the poison in their own leaves.

?
1 a) Why do some plants have spikes and thorns?
  b) Name two plants that have spikes or thorns.

2 Some goats eat African acacia trees. Suggest how they are able to do this.

3 The African acacia grows in the African savanna. Write down a food chain, with at least three steps, using this plant.

Other plants also produce poisons. Some of them, like stinging nettles, inject the poison into animals. Rabbits do not eat stinging nettles since the stings blister their sensitive noses. Some plants use mimicry to protect themselves. Deadnettles and yellow archangel plants look just like stinging nettles but they have no sting. Rabbits assume that they are stinging nettles and do not eat them.

The rash caused by stinging nettles can be relieved by rubbing with a leaf from a dock plant.

A yellow archangel plant.

4 Why do rabbits and other herbivores avoid yellow archangel plants?

5 Suggest a reason why African acacia trees only produce their poison when they have already started being eaten by a giraffe and not the whole time.

Many plants produce poisons in their leaves the whole time. The sap inside the stems of milkweed plants can cause heart attacks in small mammals. Young bracken leaves contain cyanide. Chrysanthemum plants produce a poison called pyrethrum which paralyses insects. These plants are used to make garden insecticides. The bark of the curare plant contains a poison that is used by the native people of South America to dip their arrows into. It stops some nerves working.

Chrysanthemum flowers.

The curare poison was used by Claude Bernard (1813–1878) to help develop ideas on how the nervous system works. In the 1940s it was used as an anaesthetic in hospital operations!

This insecticide is made using chemicals from chrysanthemum plants.

Many plants use substances which make them taste bad. Some contain substances called tannins which taste bitter and can stop the enzymes in the digestive system working. Chillies, which we use for cooking, contain chemicals that make them taste very hot.

Coffee contains tannins. Milky coffee tastes much less bitter than black coffee because the tannins are removed by getting stuck to proteins in the milk.

Plants are in competition with the plants around them for light, space and mineral salts. Some plants produce chemicals in their roots which stop other plants growing near them. Some plants attract ants to them by providing shelter. The ants then kill off the other plants nearby.

6 Name three ways in which humans use the defence mechanisms of plants.

7 Why do sessile oak trees produce a poison from their roots?

8 Find out how the mimosa plant protects itself.

Chemicals released from the roots of this sessile oak tree stop other plants growing near it.

What is variation?

Differences between **organisms** are known as **variation**.
There is a lot of variation between different types of animals.

A leafy sea dragon.

A wolf.

A tiger.

 1 Write down four differences between a wolf and a tiger.

There is also variation between organisms of the same type.

2 Using the photograph to help you, write a list of five things that may be different in different people.

Organisms of the same type are said to belong to the same **species**. For example, humans all belong to the same species. A species is a group of organisms that can reproduce with one another to produce new organisms (**offspring**). These offspring are also able to reproduce.

Horses and donkeys can reproduce with each other. Their offspring are called mules. However, mules cannot reproduce. This means that horses and donkeys *must* be different species.

horse

+

donkey

mule

Horses and zebras can reproduce with each other. They produce zebroids. Zebroids cannot reproduce.

Some differences are linked. For example, people with blond hair usually have blue eyes. These links are called **correlations** or **relationships**. You can often see a relationship by looking at a line graph or a bar chart. Bar charts are used to show data where one of the things you are looking at has a limited set of options. In this case either brown or blue eyes but nothing in between. We also use bar charts when looking at numbers that have been grouped together.

The bar chart shows a strong correlation between having blond hair and blue eyes because many people fall into this category. There is no relationship between having blond hair and brown eyes because there are only a few people in this category.

This line graph shows the relationship between the heights of oak trees and their masses. Line graphs are used when the numbers you measure are a range of values which change gradually. The relationship is that 'taller trees have larger masses'.

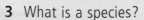

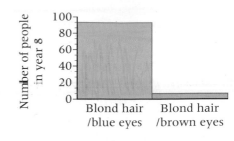

3 What is a species?

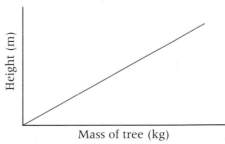

Mass of tree (kg)

P How would you find out if there is a relationship between the length of a holly leaf and the number of prickles it has?

4 a) Write down a list of five features that all humans have in common.

b) For each feature, write down whether it is exactly the same in all humans or if it can be slightly different in different people. If it can be slightly different explain how.

5 Tigers and lions can reproduce to give 'ligers'. Ligers cannot reproduce. What does this tell you about lions and tigers?

6 What relationship does this graph show?

7 Look at the two pictures below.
a) Write down two things which are the same in each.
b) Write down two things which are different in each.

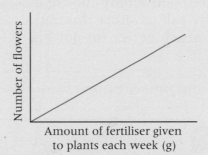

Amount of fertiliser given to plants each week (g)

You should know...

- **The word variation is used to describe the differences between organisms.**

- **Members of the same species can reproduce with each other. Their offspring are also able to reproduce.**

- **Variation occurs between different species and between members of the same species.**

- **A link between two differences is called a relationship or correlation.**

What are continuous and discontinuous variations?

If you measure the height of each person in your class, you will find that there is a range of different heights. Very few people in your class will be exactly the same height.

This variation is described as **continuous**. There is a range of values which change gradually.

If you look at the bar chart of pupils in Year 7 you can see that it is almost shaped like a bell. It shows that a lot of pupils have an average height and less pupils fall into the groups on either side.

The more pupils we measure, the more like a bell the chart becomes. The chart on the right shows the data for several thousand 12 year olds. This bell shape is known as **normal distribution**. It is called 'normal' because this is what we expect to find in things which show continuous variation.

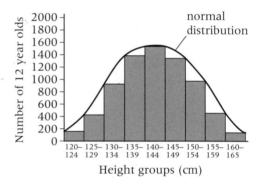

If you only measure a small number of people (a small **sample**) you may find that you do not get a bell-shaped bar chart. This is because, just by chance, you might choose a group of people who are particularly tall or short. Taking much larger sample sizes is always much better for getting more reliable results.

> **!** *Marks & Spencer measured 2500 women in the year 2000 so that they could make clothes which fitted better.*

Some people can roll their tongues and others cannot. This variation is described as being **discontinuous**. This means that there is *not* a continuous range of options.

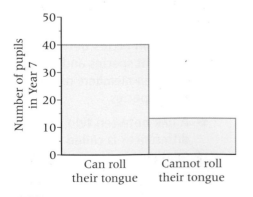

?

1 Copy the list of features below.
  a) Say whether each variation is continuous or discontinuous.
     natural eye colour   a scar
     natural hair colour   having a cold
     a tattoo   naturally curly hair
     length of hair   having pierced ears
  b) Which of these would you expect to show normal distribution?

2 a) Explain why Marks & Spencer measured so many women.
  b) What measurements do you think they took?
  c) What relationships do you think they looked for in the data?

What is inherited variation?

Children share features with their mothers and fathers but they do not look exactly like either parent. They vary.

1 a) The man in photograph D has a son.
Which of the photographs do you think shows his son? Explain your reasoning.
b) Which of the photographs do you think shows the man's mother? Explain your reasoning.

Brothers and sisters also share some features but often look very different from each other.

Half of the information needed to make a child comes from the mother and half from the father. So, children have features from both parents but the exact mixture of features in each child will be different.

We say that we **inherit** features from our parents. The variation caused by inheriting features is called **inherited variation**. The natural colour of our eyes and hair are examples of inherited variation.

2 Look at the picture on the right. Which parent has the girl inherited her hair colour from?

3 Name three features that can be inherited.

4 How much of the information needed to make a child comes from the mother?

5 Nicola's mother has blue eyes and blonde hair. Her father has brown eyes and blond hair. Both Nicola and her sister have brown eyes and blonde hair.
a) Which feature of her parents has not been passed on to either Nicola or her sister?
b) Nicola has a scar on her leg. Do you think this is an example of inherited variation? Explain your reasoning.

Eye colour and hair colour are inherited from our parents.

You should know...

● Inherited variation is caused by features being passed from parents to offspring.

How can the environment cause variation?

An organism's surroundings are called its **environment**. In all environments there are things which can change the organism. These things are called **environmental factors**.

Stinging nettle plants growing in shady areas have bigger leaves than those in sunny places. This is because they need more leaf area to trap enough sunlight for photosynthesis. The environmental factor is the amount of sunlight. The variation that this causes is the size of the leaves. Variation caused by environmental factors is called **environmental variation**.

smaller leaves where there is more light

larger leaves in the shade

 1 For each of these sentences, write down the environmental factor and the environmental variation it is causing.
  a) Bill finds the cress seedlings that he grew in a dark cupboard are yellow.
  b) Jayesh has discovered small insects on an apple tree. The tree has holes in its leaves.
  c) Rose put extra fertiliser on her sunflower plant and it is now 2 m tall.

P Algae are tiny, green organisms found in pond water. They are not plants but, like plants, they need light for photosynthesis. Fertilisers help plants to grow. How would you find out if fertilisers also help algae to grow?
• Which fertilisers would you choose?
• How would you measure how much the algae had or had not grown?

Hydrangea flowers are affected by the acidity of the soil. In acidic soils they are blue and in alkaline or neutral soils they are pink or white.

 2 Explain the meaning of each of these words:
  a) environment
  b) environmental factor
  c) environmental variation.

Environmental variation is also found in humans. The things that we do, the way that we live and what happens to us in our lives can all cause variation. Having a scar is an example of environmental variation. Something must have happened to produce a scar. Long hair is another example. In this case the environmental factor is fashion!

Some environmental factors are helpful, others are not. Good food keeps us healthy. Diseases make us ill.

3 Which of this man's features are examples of environmental variation?

4 How have environmental factors affected you, either now or in the past? Make a list of five examples.

5 This person has been in an accident involving a fire.
a) What is the environmental factor that has affected him?
b) What environmental variation has been caused?

6 Look at the pictures. What environmental factor do you think has shaped tree A?

A

B

7 a) What is the relationship between the amount of light and the size of stinging nettle leaves?
b) Sketch a graph to show this relationship.

8 Look at the picture of the hydrangea plant. What sort of soil is it growing in?

9 Copy the list of features below. For each feature, say whether it is an example of inherited variation, environmental variation or both.

natural eye colour   natural hair colour   a scar   having a cold
naturally curly hair   length of hair   a tattoo   small nose
being good at roller-blading   having pierced ears

You should know...

● An organism's surroundings are called its environment.

● There are environmental factors in an environment which cause environmental variation.

How can we describe and group things?

Throughout history, people have described variation. Whenever you read a description of a plant or animal you are reading about variation.

> The _____ started on toward the place from where the call surely came, then returned to him [Buck], sniffing noses and making actions as though to encourage him. But Buck turned about and started slowly on the back track. For the better part of an hour the wild brother ran by his side, whining softly. Then he sat down, pointed his nose upward, and howled.

A passage from a novel called Call of the Wild *by Jack London (1876–1916).*

> Imperiously he leaps, he neighs, he bounds,
>
> And now his woven girths he breaks asunder;
>
> The bearing earth with his hard hoof he wounds;
>
> Whose hollow womb resounds like
>
> heaven's thunder;
>
> The iron bit he crusheth 'tween his teeth,
>
> Controlling what he was controllèd with.

A verse from a poem called Venus and Adonis *by William Shakespeare (1564–1616).*

1 Look at the poem. What animal do you think Shakespeare was describing?

2 In the passage, Buck is a dog. The second word, which is the name of an animal, has been left out. What do you think the second word is?

Descriptions of organisms in reference books are more factual. This description is from a book used to identify insects.

3 Look at the passage about the Wood White. The name of this type of organism has been missed out. What do you think the Wood White is?

Wood White

A small delicate _____, with a wingspan of 40 mm. Basically white with greyish markings and males have black tips to forewings; no black spots. Flight is much more delicate and fluttery than Small White.

An extract from Field Guide to Insects of Britain and Northern Europe *by Bob Gibbons (Crowood Press).*

The parts of the Wood White that are being described are its wings. A description of the parts of an animal gives us a good way of telling what an animal that we have found is called. However, for the description to make sense we need to know what the parts are called.

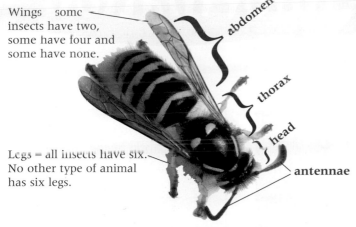

Wings – some insects have two, some have four and some have none.

abdomen

thorax

head

antennae

Legs – all insects have six. No other type of animal has six legs.

*The parts of an insect. Insect bodies have three **segments**.*

4 a) What are the names of the segments in an insect's body?

b) Which segment of an insect's body are the wings attached to?

c) You find a new animal. How could you tell that it is an insect? Choose from the following:
it has two wings
it is black and yellow
it has six legs
it has antennae.

Arachnids are another type of small animal. They have eight legs. We can put insects and arachnids into different groups based on the number of legs they have. Putting things into groups like this is called **classification**. These groups can then be used to help work out what a newly discovered organism is.

All sorts of things can be classified, even fingerprint patterns. There is a great deal of variation in fingerprints. This large amount of variation means that individual people can be identified. Everyone has a different set of fingerprints that do not change. However, fingerprints do have some common features and so can be classified. Scenes of Crime Officers look for fingerprints and compare any that they find with a chart showing the different types.

P There are three main types of fingerprint pattern. Along with others in your class, how would you try to find out what these three main types are?

- Design a chart to be used by Scenes of Crime Officers.

Compare this finger print with yours and see how much they vary.

The modern way of classifying fingerprints was developed in 1888 by the British scientist Sir Francis Galton (1822–1911). Fingerprints were first used for criminal investigations in the UK in 1901.

5 What is the proper name for grouping things together?

6 Fingerprints found at the scene of a crime cannot prove that a person committed a crime. What can they prove?

You should know...

- Organisms are classified into groups based on variations in their features.

How are animals and plants classified?

The first attempt at classifying animals according to what their parts looked like was in the 4th century BC. A Greek scientist, called Aristotle, divided animals up into two groups – those with red blood and those without red blood. Theophrastus (372–287 BC) was a pupil of Aristotle and he classified plants according to what they were used for.

Aristotle (384–322 BC).

1 What two groups did Aristotle divide animals into?

2 Suggest what two of Theophrastus' groups of plants might be called.

Aristotle and Theophrastus had only about 1000 plants and animals to classify. As more and more species were found, their groups started to contain too many organisms to be useful. An English scientist, John Ray, described nearly 19 000 plants when he started to classify organisms! Ray divided plants and animals into smaller groups. For example, he divided animals with four legs into those with hooves (e.g. cows) and those without (e.g. tigers). He then divided the animals with hooves into those with permanent horns (e.g. goats) and those which lose and regrow their horns each year (e.g. deer).

John Ray (1627–1705).

3 a) Name the three animals in the text that have hooves.
   b) A tiger does not have hooves. Name two other animals that do not have hooves.
   c) Draw a Venn diagram to show the animal groups that John Ray used.

Carl Linnaeus (1707–1778).

Today we know of about 2 000 000 different organisms and we classify them using a system invented by Carl Linnaeus in 1735. He examined tens of thousands of plants and animals and gave each one a Latin name. For example, humans are called *Homo sapiens*. Scientists all over the world use these Latin names so they do not get confused between different organisms. Common names (like robin) are confusing. What we call a robin in the UK is different to what Americans call a robin.

A British robin. Its scientific name is Erithacus rubecula.

An American robin. Its scientific name is Turdus migratorius.

Linnaeus put all the organisms into small groups of similar organisms. He then grouped the groups together. He ended up with two large groups, called **kingdoms**, which contained all the other smaller and smaller groups.

The animal kingdom can be divided into two – animals with backbones (**vertebrates**) and animals without backbones (**invertebrates**). The vertebrates are divided into five more groups. We can show these groups in a branching diagram.

4 The animal kingdom is one of the large groups in Linnaeus' system. What do you think the other large group is called?

5 Find out what the Latin words 'homo' and 'sapiens' mean.

6 Find out what these animals are:
a) *Panthera leo*
b) *Orycteropus afer*
c) *Panthera onca*
d *Sarcophilus harrisii.*

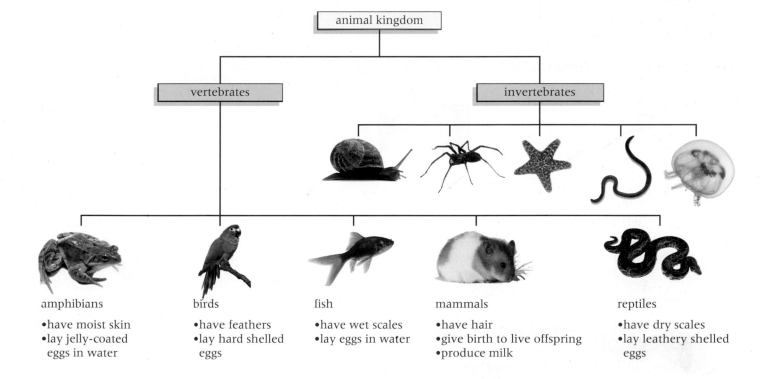

amphibians
- have moist skin
- lay jelly-coated eggs in water

birds
- have feathers
- lay hard shelled eggs

fish
- have wet scales
- lay eggs in water

mammals
- have hair
- give birth to live offspring
- produce milk

reptiles
- have dry scales
- lay leathery shelled eggs

The plant kingdom is also divided into groups. Plants and animals are not the only kingdoms. Today we use five kingdoms: plants, animals, fungi, bacteria and protoctists.

You should know…
- **How organisms are classified today.**
- **The main features of amphibians, birds, fish, mammals and reptiles.**

7 Which features are the same in birds and reptiles, and which are different?

8 a) What are animals with backbones called?
b) What groups are they divided into?
c) Write down two examples from each group.

9 Which group or groups of vertebrates:
a) do not lay eggs
b) lay eggs in water
c) have scales?

How are invertebrates classified?

Invertebrates are divided into eight more groups.

A crab is an invertebrate. It has no backbone. Its skeleton is on the outside, as this X-ray shows.

MOLLUSCS
• Crawl on a single fleshy pad

ARTHROPODS
• Have jointed legs
• Have bodies divided into sections
• Have a thick, hard outer covering

ECHINODERMS
• Have bodies divided into five parts
• Have a spiny outer covering

CNIDARIANS
• Have thin sack like bodies
• Have tentacles

ANNELIDS
• Have round, worm-like bodies
• Have bodies divided into segments

FLATWORMS
• Have flat, worm-like bodies

ROUNDWORMS
• Have long, thin, round worm-like bodies
• Have bodies with no segments

SPONGES
• Have bodies made of loosely joined cells

? 1 Copy the table and write the names of these invertebrates in the correct column.

Arthropods	Echinoderms	Molluscs

weevil   sea urchin   slug   scorpion   butterfly

crab   brittle star   fly   snail   starfish

2 Look at these animals. For each one write down which group you think it belongs to and why.

lobster   leech

3 For each of these lists of organisms, write down which is the odd one out and why.
a) snail   reindeer   pig   oak tree   sponge
b) tapeworm   slug   wasp   eagle   starfish
c) sea urchin   fly   spider   ant   lobster
d) dolphin   salmon   seagull   lobster   crocodile
e) bear   horse   pig   hamster   frog

! The longest animal ever discovered was a ribbon worm, found on a Scottish beach in 1864. It was 55 m long!

You should know...
● Invertebrates are animals without backbones.
● The main features of arthropods.

What groups can arthropods be divided into?

Scientists have identified about 800 000 different animal species on Earth. Most of these are **arthropods**. The arthropod group is divided into four smaller groups.

*A crab is a **crustacean** (pronounced 'crust-**ay**-shun'). Crustaceans have between five and seven pairs of legs. The first pair of legs are often used as pincers! Their bodies are covered in a chalky shell.*

*A spider is an **arachnid** (pronounced 'ar-**ack**-nid'). Arachnids have four pairs of legs, no wings and bodies that are divided into two sections.*

*A wasp is an **insect**. Insects have three pairs of legs and bodies that are divided into three sections. They often have wings.*

***Centipedes and millipedes** have long, thin bodies with pairs of legs on each of their many body sections.*

Although the groups are very different, all arthropods have jointed legs and a hard outer covering (called an **exoskeleton**).

1 Which group would you put scorpions into?

2 a) Why is the South American longhorn beetle classified as an arthropod?
   b) Why is it further classified as an insect?

3 Here is a list of organisms:
   butterfly, cow, crab, daffodil, eagle, snail, spider, starfish
   Using the words below, write down all the groups that each one belongs to.

amphibian	animal	annelid	arachnid	arthropod	bird
centipede	crustacean	echinoderm	fish	flatworm	insect
invertebrate	jellyfish	mammal	mollusc	plant	reptile
roundworm	sponge	vertebrate			

Nearly all arthropods lay eggs. However, scorpions give birth to live offspring.

There is a huge range of sizes for insects. South American longhorn beetles can grow up to 16 cm long. A recently discovered wasp from Guadeloupe is only 0.17 mm long.

This photograph shows a housefly to the same scale as the beetle.

You should know...

● That arthropods can be divided into smaller groups like insects and arachnids.

Where do we find acids in our food and drink?

Fizzy drinks are very popular. All these drinks have three things in common:
- they all contain a **gas** – carbon dioxide
- they all contain **sweeteners** – either sugar or artificial sweeteners
- they all contain **acids**.

Acids improve the flavour of the drinks. They balance the sweetness and make them taste 'tangy'.

 1 Name the three types of ingredients that are in fizzy drinks.
2 What is the purpose of the three ingredients?

The acid in fizzy drinks means that they can be put to all sorts of unlikely uses. Some people suggest pouring a can down the toilet to clean it, or using it to remove the rust from chrome-plated bumpers on cars. In some states in the USA, highway patrols are said to keep cola drinks in the car to remove bloodstains from the road after an accident!

These fruits all contain **citric acid**. They are called citrus fruits. The taste of lemon juice is quite sharp because of the acid. Most people prefer eating oranges to lemons, because oranges contain more natural sugar and are sweeter and less sharp. Citrus fruits also contain vitamin C, or **ascorbic acid**.

A lack of vitamin C causes scurvy. Your joints and muscles ache, your gums start bleeding and your skin and hair become very dry. British sailors had lemons and limes in their rations to stop them getting scurvy, so the Americans called them 'limeys'. Ascorbic means 'no scurvy'.

Vitamin C is also found in many green vegetables and is a vital part of our diet. Many doctors think that taking vitamin C regularly can help stop us getting colds. You are recommended to have five portions of fruit, fruit juice or vegetables each day to keep healthy. Scientific research is showing how a good balanced diet can help you concentrate better and learn more at school.

3 Name three citrus fruits.

4 What is the name of the acid in citrus fruits?

5 What is another name for vitamin C?

Vinegar is another acid that is found in many foods. As well as being put on chips, it is used in sauces, salad dressings and tomato ketchup. The scientific name for vinegar is **ethanoic acid**, though it is also known by its older name of **acetic acid**. As well as improving the taste of some foods, vinegar can also be used as a preservative. Vegetables such as onions will last longer if they are stored in vinegar. This is called pickling. The bacteria that can make the food go off cannot survive in the acid.

Can you tell which substances are acids by tasting them?

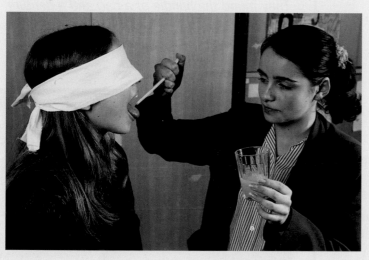

Vinegar can be made by leaving an open bottle of wine to stand. Oxygen from the air makes the wine turn acidic. Our word vinegar comes from the French 'vin aigre' – or sour wine.

6 Explain why pickled onions will keep for a longer period than normal onions.

7 a) Why isn't pickling used to preserve fruits such as strawberries?
   b) Find out about two ways of stopping fruits from being attacked by bacteria.

8 Think about your diet in a typical day.
   a) How many portions of fruit or vegetables do you eat?
   b) How might you be able to make some small changes to your meals that would give you a better balanced diet?

You should know...

● Acids have a sharp, sour taste.

● Acids can improve the taste of some foods and drinks.

● The names of some useful acids.

● Acids can preserve foods and stop them going off.

● Vinegar and fruit juices are acids.

What do hazard warning signs mean?

corrosive

irritant

Many acids are too dangerous to taste. These stronger acids can be **corrosive**. This means that they can attack metals, stonework and skin. In the laboratory, warning labels are used on bottles containing dangerous chemicals.

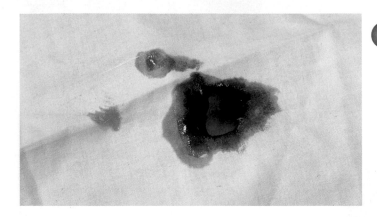

The photograph above shows what happens when **concentrated** sulphuric acid reacts with cotton. Your skin is made of similar chemicals to cotton. Most concentrated acids are highly corrosive.

The acids that you will use in the laboratory are not as dangerous as this. They have been **diluted** with water. Dilute acids will often contain between 1 and 10% acid. They are still too dangerous to taste, and could damage your eyes. These dilute acids have a hazard label with a black cross, and are classified as **irritant** or **harmful**.

Many acids are very useful in making products that we depend on every day.
- **Sulphuric acid** is used to make paints, dyes, washing up liquid and shampoo.
- **Nitric acid** is used to make fertilisers, explosives, dyes and medicines.
- **Hydrochloric acid** is used to remove rust from metals and to make important solvents.

In 1949 John Haigh was convicted of murder even though the police never found a body. He had dissolved his victim in a bath of concentrated sulphuric acid! The forensic scientists examined the sludge that remained. They found the handle of a bag and a denture, both made of plastic, which had not reacted with the acid. This was enough evidence to secure a conviction.

1 Which is more dangerous:
a) a concentrated acid or a dilute acid
b) a corrosive substance or an irritant?

2 a) Name two substances that will be attacked by a corrosive acid.
b) Name one substance that is not attacked by corrosive acids.

Acids have to be moved around the country from the factory where they are made to the place where they will be used. The tankers that carry acids have to show a hazard warning symbol, known as the Hazchem Code. This tells the public about the danger, and gives important information to the emergency services if there is an accident. The police and fire brigade need to know how to deal with any spills. They also need to know if they have to move people out of the area.

Other chemicals, such as alkalis, are also dangerous, and will carry warning symbols as well. If you spill some acid or alkali on your skin, wash it off with plenty of water. Water dilutes the acid or alkali and makes it less dangerous. Whenever you use acids or alkalis, you must wear eye protection because they can cause severe eye damage.

 How could you compare different acids to see which is the most hazardous?

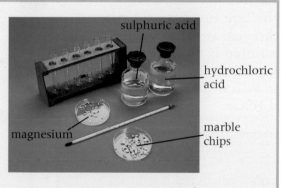

sulphuric acid

hydrochloric acid

magnesium

marble chips

3 Name four acids.

4 Give two examples of where acids are useful.

5 Make a leaflet or a poster which shows how you should handle acids and alkalis safely in the laboratory, and the precautions that you should take.

6 Acids are usually transported in concentrated form, even though this is more dangerous. Why do you think this is?

7 Imagine that there has been an acid tanker crash on a road near to where you live. Write a newspaper report of the incident, explaining some of the actions that the police and fire services would have taken.

You should know...

● **Many acids are dangerous.**

● **Dangerous chemicals *must* have a warning symbol on them.**

● **Corrosive acids are the most dangerous.**

● **Irritant acids are less dangerous.**

What is an indicator?

Many flowers and fruits have bright colours and many coloured dyes can be obtained from them.

Some dyes can change colour when they mix with certain chemicals. A dye which can change colour is called an **indicator**. One example is **litmus**. This can be red or blue, or sometimes purple (blue and red together). You can also get litmus paper, which changes colour in the same way.

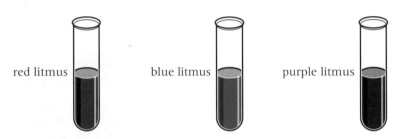

red litmus   blue litmus   purple litmus

Acids always turn litmus red. If you are not sure whether a substance is an acid or not, you can test it using litmus. If the litmus turns red, the mystery substance is an acid. If the litmus stays purple, or turns blue, then it is not an acid. Other things which change colour when they are mixed with acids include blackberry juice and tea.

1 Name three indicators.

2 What colour would purple litmus go if you mixed it with:
   a) sulphuric acid
   b) tap water
   c) lemon juice?

3 A few drops of litmus solution were added to some toothpaste. The litmus turned blue. What does this tell us about toothpaste?

4 Sally crushed up some purple berries from a bush, and mixed them with a little water. When she mixed the juice with some washing powder, it changed colour to red.
   a) Is the berry juice acting as an indicator? Explain your answer.
   b) Which of these best describes the washing powder?
      A definitely an acid
      B definitely not an acid
      C possibly an acid
      Explain your answer.

How could you see if red cabbage worked as an indicator?
• What would you do to the leaves to get the colour out?
• How could you separate the coloured juice from the leaves?

You should know...

● Indicators have a definite colour when mixed with acids.

● Litmus is an indicator which is red in acids.

Making an ash of it

What is an alkali?

In ancient times, Arabic scientists took ashes from fires and mixed them with water. This liquid was boiled with animal fats to make the first soap. In Arabic, the ashes were called 'al kali'. We use the word **alkali** to describe a group of substances that feel soapy. However, many alkalis are too dangerous to feel.

In some ways, alkalis are the opposite of acids. They make indicators go a different colour. Alkalis turn litmus blue.

Many substances are neither acids nor alkalis. These are called **neutral**. Pure water, and salt and sugar solutions are all neutral. Neutral substances do not affect indicators at all.

 Alkalis feel soapy because they can start to react with the natural oils in your skin. Your skin can start to turn into soap! Oven cleaners often contain alkalis. The grease in the oven is attacked by the cleaner, and turns into soap. This helps the cleaning process.

 How could you use this colour chart for litmus to find out if something is an acid, an alkali or neutral?
- What apparatus would you use?

| acid | neutral | alkali |

 1 An indicator called methyl orange turns red in acid, and yellow in alkali.
   a) What colour would this indicator turn with grapefruit juice?
   b) What colour would it turn with oven cleaner?

Alkalis and acids cancel each other out to make neutral substances. For example, toothpastes contain a mild alkali to get rid of some of the acid in your mouth.

 2 What is a 'neutral' substance?

3 State whether these substances are acid, alkali or neutral:
   a) vinegar   b) water   c) salt
   d) lemon juice e) toothpaste f) sugar
   g) soap.

You should know...
- Litmus turns blue in alkalis.
- Alkalis can cancel out acids, making them neutral.
- Some alkalis are dangerous.

How can we make a better indicator?

Litmus can show us whether something is an acid, an alkali or neutral. However, simple indicators like this cannot tell us whether an acid or alkali is strong or weak.

To find this out, we use a mixture of indicators to give a range of different colours. This mixture is called **universal indicator** and it will go a certain colour depending on the strength of the acid or alkali.

Universal indicator comes as a liquid or as test papers. It gives the same range of colours as a rainbow: red, orange, yellow, green, blue and purple. We can use it to place substances on a numbered scale which runs from 1 to 14. This is known as the **pH scale**.

1 a) What is universal indicator?
b) What is it used for?

In 1909 Søren Peter Sørensen, a Danish chemist, designed the pH scale in an effort to control the quality of beer manufacture.

strong acid			weak acid			neutral	weak alkali			strong alkali			
1	2	3	4	5	6	7	8	9	10	11	12	13	14

stomach acid — vinegar — skin — pure water — indigestion powders — washing powder — oven cleaner

lemon juice — fizzy drinks — milk — blood — toothpaste

pHs of different substances.

2 a) What pH number would a substance have if it turned universal indicator red?
b) Would it be an acid or an alkali?
c) Would it be strong or weak?

Many skin products now advertise their pH value. Your skin is naturally slightly acidic; it has a pH of about 5.5. Most soaps are alkaline, with a pH of about 9 or 10. Some people find that using soap can dry out their skin and so some manufacturers have now developed alternatives that match the pH of skin.

Most shampoos and shower gels are slightly acidic, though they may not all match the pH of skin precisely.

3 What colour would a soap with a pH of 5.5 turn universal indicator?

 P How could you find out the pHs of different skin products?
● What apparatus would you need?

The hydrochloric acid in your stomach has a pH of 1 or 2.
This acid helps to break down your food. If you produce too much acid, you may suffer from indigestion, or heartburn.

Remedies like Milk of Magnesia are called **antacids**. They contain alkalis to cancel out some of the acid. The alkalis are weak, so that they do not make your stomach too alkaline. Indigestion remedies are usually about pH 9.

 4 a) What is 'heartburn'?
b) What can be done to relieve the symptoms?
c) Why does this work?

5 What is the pH of:
a) stomach acid   b) pure water
c) skin   d) Milk of Magnesia
e) soap?

6 Copy and complete the following table:

Name of chemical	Colour of universal indicator	Acid, alkali or neutral	pH
Hydrochloric acid		Strong acid	
			7
Milk of Magnesia			
Sodium hydroxide	Purple		
Carbon dioxide solution		Weak acid	

7 Find out about the use of acids and alkalis in one of these situations. Choose from:
a) hair and skin care   b) stings and bites
c) treating indigestion   d) preserving food
e) treatment of soil.

pH
14
13
12
11
10
9
8
7
6
5
4
3
2
1
0

This means that the substance attacks and damages things including skin and eyes.

This means that the substance can make your skin blister or become itchy.

Strong acids and alkalis are more corrosive than weak acids or alkalis.

You should know...

● The strengths of acids and alkalis can be measured on the pH scale.

● pH numbers 1 to 6 are acids, 7 is neutral, and 8 to 14 are alkalis.

● You can find out the pH number using universal indicator.

What happens when an acid is added to an alkali?

Insect stings can be very painful. A bee sting is acidic. It has a pH of about 3.5. To stop a bee sting hurting you can add a weak alkali. The alkali will **neutralise** the acid. The pH of the affected area will become closer to the natural pH of the body. Wasp stings are alkaline – about pH 10. They need to be neutralised with a weak acid.

1 a) What is the pH of a bee sting?
   b) Is this acidic, alkaline or neutral?

2 Bicarbonate of soda solution has a pH of about 9. Why is this a good thing to treat a bee sting with?

3 a) What type of substance would you use to treat a wasp sting?
   b) If someone was in your kitchen and got stung by a wasp, suggest something that you could find in your food cupboard to put on to the sting to relieve the pain.

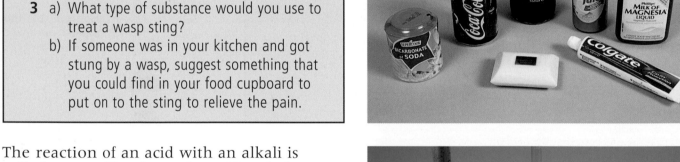

The reaction of an acid with an alkali is called **neutralisation**. The acid and the alkali neutralise one another. If exactly the right amounts are added, you will end up with a neutral solution.

The change in pH during neutralisation can be measured using this apparatus. The beaker contains sodium hydroxide solution, with a few drops of universal indicator solution. Acid can be added a little at a time from a **burette**. Each time the acid is added, you can measure the pH. You can match the colour that the universal indicator goes to a pH colour chart. You can also use a piece of apparatus called a pH meter to measure pHs.

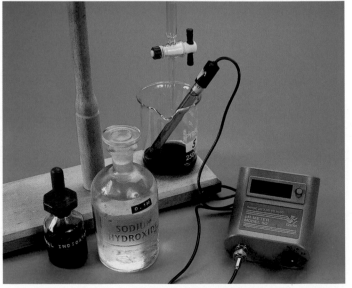

4 a) What is the colour of the universal indicator in the photograph on page 64?
b) What pH is the sodium hydroxide solution?

5 When just enough acid has been added to neutralise the sodium hydroxide:
a) what will the pH be
b) what colour will the indicator be?

6 If you carry on adding more acid:
a) what colour will the indicator change to
b) what will happen to the pH?

Another way of changing the pH of an acid or alkali is by **diluting** it. If you add more water, the pH will get closer to 7. Adding 9 volumes of water to 1 volume of an acid or alkali will change the pH by 1 unit.

In many situations it is important to get the balance right.

Some plants grow best in soils of a certain pH. Gardeners add lime to the soil if it is too acidic.

Many foods contain acids which help to preserve them, but too much acid would make them taste bad. They would also be dangerous to eat.

Our bodies have developed control mechanisms for keeping the pH constant in our blood and digestive system. Sometimes we need to take medicines to help keep the balance right.

 Which indigestion remedy works best? Indigestion tablets cancel out acid in the stomach.
- How could you find out which indigestion tablets are best?

Make sure that you carry out a safe investigation!

7 Why would it not be a good idea to use a solution of sodium hydroxide (pH 13) to neutralise the acid in a bee sting?

8 Would toothpaste be more effective at treating a bee sting or a wasp sting? Explain your answer.

You should know...

- A neutral solution can be made by adding an acid to an alkali.

- When an acid is added to an alkali, the pH of the alkali is lowered.

- Diluting an acid or an alkali will bring the pH closer to 7.

How do we know when a chemical reaction has occurred?

If you melt ice it turns into water. The ice has changed state but it is still the same substance. This is called a **physical change**. No new substances are formed. The change is **reversible** since the water can easily be turned back into ice.

Some changes are not physical changes because a new substance is formed. Changes that produce a new substance are called **chemical reactions**.

 1 Is water turning into steam a physical change or a chemical reaction?

Chemical reactions are happening all around us. Some are useful and some are not useful. Sometimes it is obvious that there is a reaction taking place. For instance, in a firework display, you can see the colours and the smoke, and hear the bangs. However, not all reactions are as obvious as this.

 2 What do you see which shows that a reaction has taken place when fireworks go off?

There are three observations which can tell you whether a chemical reaction has occurred:
- there may be a change in colour
- a gas may be given off
- there may be an energy change (for example, the mixture may get hotter).

When a firework goes off, you can't collect all the gases and smoke and turn them back into a firework. This is a **permanent** or **irreversible** change. New substances have been formed. In a chemical reaction a new substance is formed and it is usually very difficult to reverse the reaction.

P

When you mix chemicals together, how do you tell if a reaction has taken place?
- What will you look for?
- What other senses could you use, apart from sight?

 3 Write down three observations which tell us that a chemical change has taken place.

4 What is the difference between a chemical reaction and a physical change?

Some reactions occur as soon as two chemicals are mixed. Other reactions need energy to start them off. When you cook food, the heat from the cooker makes chemical reactions happen in the food. These reactions cause different changes in different foods.

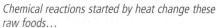

Chemical reactions started by heat change these raw foods…

… into these cooked foods.

5 How do you know a chemical reaction has happened when these foods are cooked:
a) eggs   b) meat   c) onions?

Some food changes on its own, without being heated. Fruit is often picked before it is ripe and ready to eat. Chemical reactions inside the fruit continue after it is picked, and ripen it.

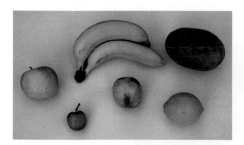

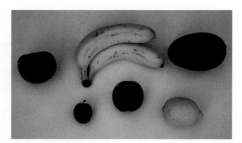

Fruit growers can speed up ripening by using a gas called ethene. Bananas give off a lot of this gas, so if you want some fruit to ripen quickly, put a banana in with it!

6 Look carefully at the photographs of the ripening fruit. The apple has changed from a pale green to a deep reddish brown. Write down four other observations which show that chemical reactions have taken place.

You should know...

● In a chemical change a new substance is formed.

● Most chemical changes are permanent (irreversible).

● In a physical change, no new substance is formed.

● Physical changes are usually reversible.

How do acids react with metals?

Rusting is a slow chemical reaction. The parts of this moped that are made of iron and steel have reacted with oxygen and water in the air. They have turned into **rust** (iron oxide). Rusting is an example of **corrosion**.

 1 How can you tell that a reaction has occurred when iron rusts?

Acids can be **corrosive**. Sometimes rainwater may be polluted with nitric or sulphuric acids. This **acid rain** will attack the iron and make it corrode more quickly.

 2 a) Which of the two bottles of acid shown on the right is more dangerous?
 b) How can you tell this from the hazard labels?
 c) Which acid is mostly water?

concentrated sulphuric acid

This means that the substance attacks and damages things including skin and eyes.

corrosive

This means that the substance can make your skin blister or become itchy.

Dilute sulphuric acid

irritant

The magnesium in this tube reacts quickly with the sulphuric acid. The magnesium and sulphuric acid are called the **reactants**. Bubbles of hydrogen gas are given off. Hydrogen is a **product** in this reaction. We can test for hydrogen by bringing a lighted splint up to the tube. The gas burns with a squeaky pop. This shows that it is hydrogen. At the end of the reaction there is no metal left – it has all been corroded away and turned into a new substance.

 3 In the reaction between magnesium and sulphuric acid, name:
 a) a metal   **b)** a gas
 c) a reactant   **d)** a product.

You should know...

● Acids can react with some metals to produce hydrogen.

● Hydrogen burns with a squeaky pop.

● In a chemical reaction, reactants turn into products.

P How can you find out which metals and acids react together to make hydrogen?

Fizz and chips

How do acids react with carbonates?

Over the years, the limestone in the picture has been corroded by a chemical reaction with the rain. Weak acid in the rain has attacked and corroded the limestone and changed it into a new substance which is soluble. When acids react with limestone (calcium carbonate), **carbon dioxide** gas is given off. You can test this reaction in the laboratory using the limestone chips that are often mixed with tarmac in road surfaces or drives. Other carbonates will react in a similar way.

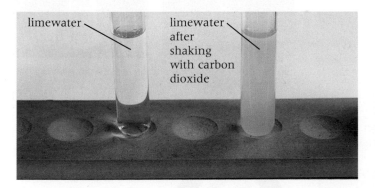

Carbon dioxide is also the gas in fizzy drinks. If you open a bottle of fizzy drink, it will often 'froth up' as the carbon dioxide escapes from the liquid.

 P How can you find out which rocks and indigestion remedies contain carbonates?

If you put a lighted splint into carbon dioxide the flame goes out straight away. This means that you can easily tell the difference between carbon dioxide and hydrogen. Other gases will also put the flame out. To be sure that a gas is carbon dioxide we use the **limewater** test. If carbon dioxide is mixed with limewater, the limewater will go milky. With other gases, the limewater stays clear.

?
1 What is the name of the gas in fizzy drinks? ·

2 Copy and complete these sentences using words from the list.
   clear   cloudy   colourless   white
   a) Before carbon dioxide is added, limewater is _____ and _____.
   b) After carbon dioxide is added, limewater is _____ and _____.

3 Describe what tests you would do to tell the difference between:
   a) carbon dioxide and hydrogen
   b) carbon dioxide and oxygen.

limewater

limewater after shaking with carbon dioxide

You should know...

● Acids react with carbonates to produce carbon dioxide.

● Carbon dioxide turns limewater milky.

● Some rocks and indigestion remedies contain carbonates.

What new materials are made when things burn?

Oxygen is a gas found in the air. It is one of the reactants in many chemical reactions.

Some metals react with oxygen when they are heated together with the gas. Some of these metals burn and give out great amounts of heat energy, others do not.

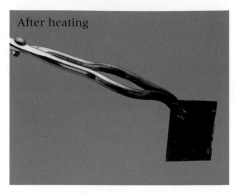
Before heating

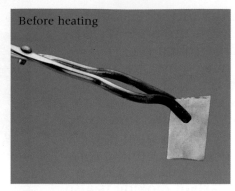
After heating

Copper does not burn …

… but becomes black when it is heated.

1 a) Which gas is needed for things to burn?
   b) Where does this gas come from?

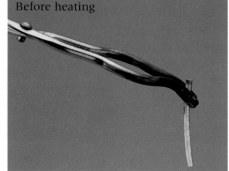
Before heating

After heating

Magnesium burns and forms a white ash.

You can see the white ash on the tongs.

When the metals react with oxygen, they combine with it and form new substances called **oxides**. When magnesium reacts with the oxygen, it makes magnesium oxide. We can write down what happens in this reaction in a **word equation**. A word equation summarises what happens in a reaction.

magnesium + oxygen ⟶ magnesium oxide
reactants   product

Metals which burn will burn more brightly in pure oxygen.

Iron hardly burns when it is in air. In pure oxygen it burns brightly.

2 a) What will be made when copper reacts with oxygen?
   b) Write a word equation for the reaction between copper and oxygen.

3 Write a word equation for the reaction between iron and oxygen.

The three things needed for something to burn are shown in the Fire Triangle. The fuel is the substance that is burning.

Fire can be very useful. It can cook food and keep us warm. It can be used to cut holes in metal, and it can help us to celebrate special events.

A **fuel** is a substance which contains a store of **chemical energy** which can be changed into other forms of energy. Wood, coal, oil, petrol and natural gas are all fuels.

 4 a) What is a fuel?
  b) What fuel is used in the cooker in the picture above?

The fuel in the bonfire will not burn unless it is heated first. A flame is used to give the bonfire some heat energy. The bonfire also needs oxygen from the air. If there is no oxygen, the fuel cannot burn so there will be no fire.

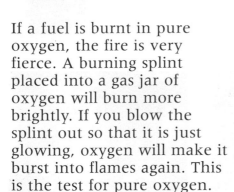

This bonfire is made from wood, which is a kind of fuel.

The fuel and oxygen are used up when the bonfire burns.

If a fuel is burnt in pure oxygen, the fire is very fierce. A burning splint placed into a gas jar of oxygen will burn more brightly. If you blow the splint out so that it is just glowing, oxygen will make it burst into flames again. This is the test for pure oxygen.

 5 Charcoal is mostly carbon. Suggest the name of a new substance that could be formed when charcoal burns.

A glowing splint put into a jar of oxygen.

 6 How could you use the lighted splint test to tell the difference between test tubes of hydrogen, oxygen and carbon dioxide?

You should know...

- Metals react with oxygen to make metal oxides.

- A fire will only burn if fuel, heat and oxygen are present.

- When a substance burns, it combines with oxygen from the air.

How do you put out a fire?

A fire will only burn if fuel, heat and oxygen are present. Once it is lit, a fire will continue to burn until one of these three things runs out. The things needed for a fire to burn are shown in the **Fire Triangle**.

To put out a fire, you need to take away one of the three sides of the fire triangle. Fire extinguishers work by cooling the fire, or by stopping oxygen getting to the fuel.

> **?** **1** Describe two ways that a fire extinguisher can put out a fire.

There are different types of fire extinguisher. It is important to choose the right type of fire extinguisher for each type of fire. Using the wrong type of extinguisher on a fire may be dangerous and can even make the fire spread.

Water is often used to put out fires because it takes away the heat. However, water should never be used when petrol or oil is burning as the water makes the burning fuel spread out.

The water sinks through the oil, and the heat from the fire turns the water into steam. The steam rises very quickly to the surface of the oil, pushing the burning oil out of the way. This makes the burning oil and the fire spread out.

The best way to put out a petrol or oil fire is to cover it with a thick layer of something (e.g. sand, earth or a fire blanket) to keep the air away.

Type of extinguisher	Type of fire used on
Water	Wood, paper, cloth
Carbon dioxide	Electrical fires
AFFF (Aqueous Film Forming Foam)	Wood, paper, petrol, solvents, paints, plastics
Dry powder	Fires involving metals

A chip pan fire … *… with water added!*

> **?** **2** Why should you never put water onto an oil fire?

Water should never be put onto anything which is electrical as it may give you a serious electric shock. Turn off the electricity at the mains, and use sand or a dry powder fire extinguisher to stop air getting to the fire. A dry powder extinguisher smothers the flames by covering them in a fine layer of powder.

3 a) Why should you not put water on an electrical fire?

b) What should you use instead?

When a plane crashes, foam can be sprayed onto it to make sure the fuel doesn't catch fire. The foam stops oxygen from reaching the fuel.

Some fires are too big to put out using extinguishers. If there is a forest fire it can be very difficult to stop it spreading. Forests often have wide gaps between some of the trees. These areas without trees are called 'fire breaks'. The fire will run out of fuel when it reaches a 'fire break'. This will stop the fire from spreading any further.

Foam can be used to stop a fire from starting.

4 a) What is a fire break?

b) How does it help to put out a forest fire?

A fire break can stop a forest fire spreading.

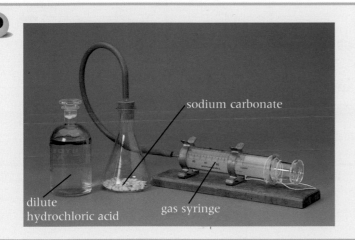
sodium carbonate

dilute hydrochloric acid

gas syringe

Some fire extinguishers work by releasing a stream of carbon dioxide gas which forms a layer over the fire and stops oxygen from reaching the flames. A model fire extinguisher can be made by adding dilute acid to sodium carbonate.
- How much carbonate must you add to some dilute acid to make the most carbon dioxide gas?
- Try to make the most carbon dioxide using the smallest amount of acid.

Fires naturally break out in forest areas, started by lightning in dry weather. People who look after the forest let these small fires burn out. This helps to stop very large fires happening, as some of the fuel has been used up.

5 Design a poster or a leaflet to explain how to put out different types of fire.

6 Why do you think that letting small fires burn in forests helps to stop large fires happening?

What is produced when fuels burn?

When a candle burns, a **chemical reaction** takes place. Candles are made from wax. Wax is a substance which contains a lot of carbon joined to hydrogen. When a candle burns, the carbon joins with oxygen from the air to make a new substance, called an **oxide**. This new compound is carbon dioxide.

The wax also has a lot of hydrogen in it. The hydrogen joins with oxygen to make another oxide, hydrogen oxide. Hydrogen oxide is better known as water. These oxides are new chemicals and we cannot get the candle wax back again. The reaction cannot be reversed. It is **irreversible**.

1 What is made when carbon joins with oxygen?

2 What does 'irreversible' mean?

P How could you show that water, carbon dioxide and heat are produced when different fuels are burnt?

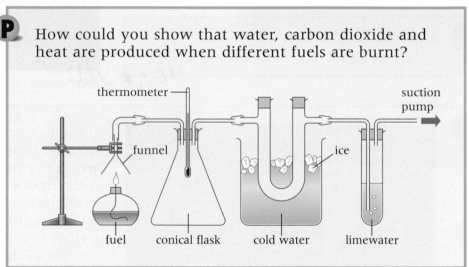

thermometer — suction pump — funnel — ice — fuel — conical flask — cold water — limewater

Burning is more properly called **combustion**. It is an example of a **combination reaction**. A combination reaction takes place when one substance joins with another substance. The carbon joins with oxygen and the hydrogen joins with oxygen.

3 What is a combination reaction?

We can summarise what happens when we burn a fuel by writing a word equation:

fuel + oxygen ⟶ carbon dioxide + water (+ energy)

Energy is in brackets in this equation because it is not a chemical substance and so it is *not* a product. It is not usually written in a word equation.

4 a) What are the reactants in this reaction?
b) What are the products?

Natural gas is another example of a fuel. Natural gas is mainly methane. Methane is a substance which contains carbon and hydrogen. Any chemical which is made of only carbon and hydrogen is called a **hydrocarbon**. When methane burns, it reacts with the oxygen in the air to make carbon dioxide and water. Heat and light energy are released.

methane + oxygen ⟶ carbon dioxide + water (+ energy)

If there is not enough oxygen, the methane cannot burn properly. When this happens, some of the carbon combines with a little oxygen to form carbon monoxide. Some carbon will not react with oxygen at all, and forms carbon powder, often called soot.

methane + a little oxygen ⟶ carbon monoxide + carbon + water (+ energy)

5 Why is it important to make sure gas fires have enough oxygen to burn methane completely?

This can be dangerous because carbon monoxide is a very poisonous gas. Gas fires should be serviced properly to make sure that they get enough oxygen and do not make carbon monoxide. We can test for carbon monoxide by placing a carbon monoxide detector near to gas appliances. We need to use a detector because we cannot smell or taste carbon monoxide.

Methane is not the only gas which burns. The large external tank on the space shuttle contains hydrogen, which it uses as a fuel. Another tank contains oxygen, so that the fuel can burn. The hydrogen joins with oxygen to form water, and a lot of energy is released.

6 Some fuels are more difficult to burn than others. Name one fuel which burns easily and one fuel which is difficult to burn. Which would be safer to use to power a car? Explain your choice.

7 a) What fuel is used on the space shuttle?
   b) Write a word equation for the chemical reaction which takes place when the space shuttle takes off.

You should know...
● Burning is a chemical reaction which forms oxides.
● fuel + oxygen → carbon dioxide + water (+ energy)

Explosives

What are explosives and what are they used for?

When a chemical releases a large amount of energy very quickly, an explosion occurs. An explosion is a chemical reaction which causes huge amounts of gases to be formed. A lot of heat is also released.

 1 What types of energy are released in an explosion?

These chemical reactions need oxygen. Sometimes the oxygen comes from the air, and sometimes a substance contains enough oxygen for the reaction to happen without needing air. If the reaction needs oxygen from the air, it is a **combustion** reaction. If it does not need oxygen from the air, it is a **decomposition** reaction.

 2 Some chemicals explode by combustion and others by decomposition. What is the difference between the two types of explosion?

The gas in this cylinder exploded in a fire. The cylinder was thrown hundreds of feet into the air.

Chemicals which are designed to explode are called **explosives**. However, even everyday chemicals can explode. Natural gas will explode if it is mixed with the right amount of oxygen and heated to a high temperature.

Exploding natural gas was a problem for coal miners in the 18th century. While cutting away at the coal, large amounts of methane were often released which exploded due to the high temperatures of the flames in the lamps they used.

In 1815, Sir Humphry Davy invented a safer mining lamp called the Davy lamp. A wire mesh around the flame inside the lamp conducted heat away from the flame making the surrounding air less hot. This stopped the natural gas exploding.

The Davy lamp.

 3 Do you think methane explodes by combustion or decomposition? Explain your answer.

4 Why do you think a metal mesh is used in a Davy lamp and not one made out of glass?

Explosions often cause fires. Explosive chemicals can also be used to put out fires! An oil well is a non-stop supply of fuel. Explosives can be used to blow out the flames and the blast of air cools the oil enough to let the oil workers stop the leak.

 Red Adaire is an American fire fighter who puts out oil well fires by blowing them up with explosives.

An oil well fire.

Explosives are also used to blast rock out of quarries, build roads through hills, knock down old buildings quickly, and for fireworks.

For a long time, the only explosive available was gunpowder. This was invented in China about 1200 years ago. Gunpowder is not very powerful. It needs to be lit with a flame and the explosion goes through the powder at a speed of about 60 m/s.

Gunpowder is still used in fireworks.

In 1847, an Italian Scientist, Ascanio Sobrero, invented nitroglycerine. An explosion spreads through this liquid at 7000 m/s! It is also very dangerous – it explodes with even the slightest knock. Chemicals like this are described as **unstable**.

5 Write down as many uses for explosives as you can think of.

In 1865, Alfred Nobel opened a factory to make nitroglycerine. The factory blew up, killing his brother. Nobel went on to invent a more stable form of this explosive, by soaking the nitroglycerine in a type of clay. This was called dynamite.

Dynamite is still used today. There are also many other explosives which, like dynamite, are very powerful but also very stable.

'Plastic explosives' are not made out of plastic! The name refers to one of their properties – they can be moulded into shape.

The power of explosives is due to the speed with which the chemical reaction occurs, not the amount of energy inside the chemical. Many breakfast cereals contain about 1600 kJ/100g. The explosive, TNT, contains 1500 kJ/100g!

6 These pictures show three types of explosive. Write down what you think their names are.

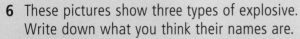

A   B   C
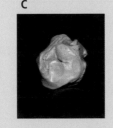

7 Nitroglycerine is an explosive compound made up of the elements carbon, hydrogen, oxygen and nitrogen. When it decomposes, it produces many different gases. Suggest what some of these gases might be.

8 Why do you think dynamite is more widely used than nitroglycerine?

9 Find out what detonators are and why they are often needed.

What are the differences between solids, liquids and gases?

Solids, liquids and gases are the three **states of matter**. We can tell solids, liquids and gases apart by looking at how each material behaves. The materials have different **properties**.

Solids

This lorry is specially designed to carry a large bulky **solid** load. Once this turbine has been built, it has a shape that cannot be changed easily. The turbine cannot be easily squashed into a smaller space.

Solids also tend to stay in one place unless they are pushed or pulled. Once a solid object has been loaded onto a lorry, it stays there because a solid doesn't **flow**.

The turbine in the picture at the top of the page is very heavy for its size. We say that any object which is heavy for its volume is **dense**. Solids are often dense.

 1 Write down the three properties of solids.

Liquids

It would be very difficult to transport water in the aquarium. The aquarium would be very heavy and the water would slosh about as it was moved. This shows us one of the important properties of **liquids** – they **flow**.

Some liquids flow more easily than others. For example, water flows more easily than treacle.

Liquids cannot be squashed. Liquids are quite dense, but they are usually less dense than solids.

 2 How would you carry the fish home so that they didn't end up without any water?

If we want to carry a liquid, like water, we need a sealed container. If we want to carry water or milk around the country we use a tanker.

All liquids can be pumped into and out of tankers because the liquids can change shape. This means that a tanker can be filled and sent to the place where the liquid is needed, without spilling a drop.

 3 Write down the properties of liquids.

Gases

This diver has to carry all the air that she will need to breathe during her dive. The small cylinder on her back contains enough air to let her stay under the water for about an hour.

In one day, a person normally breathes the volume of air contained in a small room. We can only get all this air into a small cylinder if we squash it.

Air is a mixture of gases, and all gases can be squashed.

When we squash a gas, we make its volume smaller. Gases do not have a fixed volume – they fill the whole of the space they are in. When we put the gas into the cylinder, we change its shape and its volume.

Large amounts of a gas can be transported by squashing it into a tank.

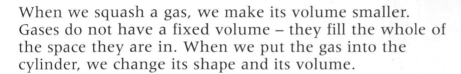

 4 Make a list of all the properties of gases.

5 What are the differences between solids, liquids and gases? Make a list of as many differences as you can. Make a table to show your answers:

Solids	Liquids	Gases
fixed shape		
	fixed volume	

6 A friend of yours thinks that sand is a liquid! Is he right? (*Hint:* Think about the properties of liquids and solids. For example are there any differences between a single grain of sand and a lorry load of sand?)

You should know…

- Solids are difficult to squash, do not flow, have a fixed shape and volume, and have a high density.

- Liquids cannot be squashed, flow quite easily, and have a fixed volume but no fixed shape.

- Although they are dense, liquids often have a lower density than solids.

- Gases are easy to squash, flow easily, have no fixed volume and no fixed shape.

- Gases have a lower density than liquids.

What is a theory?

Science is about trying to *explain* the world around us.
One of the things scientists have tried to explain is why a
substance behaves differently if it is a solid, a liquid or a gas.

Scientists collect **data** or **observations**. Some observations
about solids are:
• solids usually keep the same shape
• solids are difficult to squash.

Scientists think about the observations, and try to find an
idea that explains them. They often have to use their
imaginations. For instance, you might try to explain what
happens when ice melts by imagining that you have a really
powerful microscope that can see inside the ice.

> **1** Write down two
> observations about
> liquids. (*Hint:* you may
> need to look back at
> pages 78 and 79).

Observation: if you heat ice, it disappears and water runs away from it.

Idea: ice is made of lots of little boxes with water in them. The heat breaks the boxes open, so the water can run out.

> **2** Look at the cartoon.
>   a) What is the
>   observation that this
>   person is trying to
>   explain?
>   b) What is his idea?

Scientists can never really know if their
idea is right. A good idea is one that
explains a lot of evidence. It can also be
used to make **predictions** about what
will happen in other experiments. These
predictions can then be tested.

If an idea has been tested and still works,
it is usually called a **theory**.

> **3** Look at the cartoon again.
>   a) Write down three more things that the idea
>   about solids, liquids and gases would have
>   to explain. (*Hint:* you may need to look back
>   at pages 78 and 79).
>   b) How well does the idea explain these things?
>   c) Why do you think scientists do not believe
>   the idea?

One of the most important ideas in science explains the differences between solids and gases. This theory also explains a lot of other observations.

It is very difficult to squash a solid or a liquid. It is quite easy to squash a gas.

solid   liquid   gas

If you heat a sealed container, it will explode.

If you put a purple crystal into water, it starts to dissolve and turn the water purple. If you leave the water long enough, the purple spreads out through the water *without stirring*.

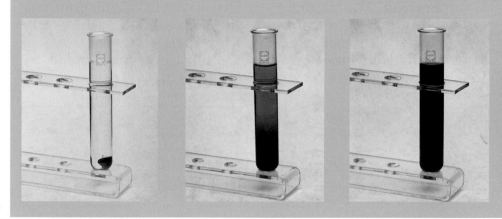

You can make an orange drink using squash and water. The colour and flavour spread out. If you add more water, you **dilute** the drink. If you add enough water, you will not be able to see the orange colour any more.

4 a) What is an observation?
   b) What is a theory?
   c) What is a prediction?

5 Write down three things that a theory about solids, liquids and gases should be able to explain.

You should know…

● The differences between an observation, a theory and a prediction.

● Some of the things that a theory about solids, liquids and gases should be able to explain.

What is particle theory?

Particle theory can explain the properties of solids, liquids and gases. This theory says that all things are made of tiny pieces called **particles**. Solids, liquids and gases have different arrangements of particles. This gives them their special properties.

1 What are all materials made from?

Solids have particles that are close together. The particles are fixed in place and cannot swap places with each other. That is why solids have a fixed shape.

The particles in a liquid are still attached to one another, but so weakly that they can move past each other. Liquids can change shape.

In gases, the particles are not attached to each other and can move anywhere by themselves. Gases can also change shape.

solid

liquid

gas

2 What decides whether a material is a solid, liquid or gas?

Explaining the properties

Things can only change their volume if the particles in them spread out or get closer together. In a solid, the particles are already very close together. This makes it very difficult for the volume of a solid to be made smaller.

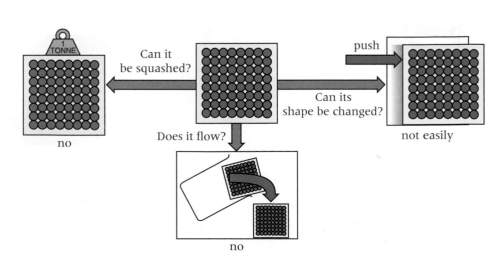

Can it be squashed? no

push Can its shape be changed? not easily

Does it flow? no

Solids have a fixed shape because the particles are held tightly together by special forces called **bonds**. These bonds are very strong, and they stop the particles from moving around. The particles are fixed in place and can only **vibrate**. This stops the whole solid from flowing.

3 What holds the particles together in a solid?

The volume of a liquid cannot be changed. Liquids cannot be squashed because the particles in a liquid are already close together.

The particles in a liquid are close together but they can move past each other quite easily. The bonds in a liquid are weak enough to let the particles move about but strong enough to hold them close together.

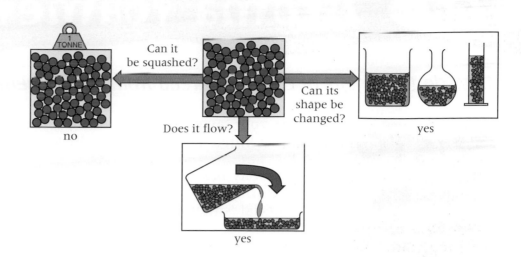

Particles in a gas are very far apart and move very quickly in all directions. The particles are able to move all over the place because there are no bonds between them. Therefore, a gas does not have a fixed volume or shape.

When we squash a gas, the particles are moved closer together. The more the gas is squashed, the closer together the particles will get.

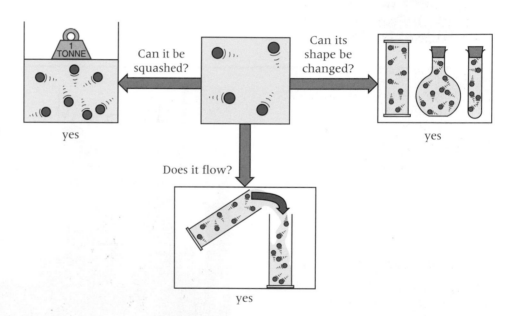

4 What happens to the particles if air is squashed into a smaller space?

5 Why are gas particles able to spread out to fill any space?

6 Why is it very difficult to squash solids and liquids?

7 Describe how the particles move in solids, liquids and gases.

You should know...

● Materials have different properties because they are made from particles which are arranged in different ways, making a solid, liquid or gas.

● Solids are made up of particles that are very close together.

● Liquids are made up of particles that are fairly close together.

● Gases are made up of particles that are far apart.

How do the smells of cooking spread from the kitchen?

Imagine your favourite food is being cooked in the kitchen. The smell can make you hungry. But how does the smell get to you?

Some 'smelly particles' are given off by the food. These particles then spread through the air. Some of them end up in your nose where you have special 'smell detectors'.

Even if the air is not moving, you will still notice the smell. This is because the gas particles are moving on their own. The way that a smell moves around a room like this is called **diffusion**. The 'smelly particles' are mixing with the air particles without anything moving them.

How could you measure the speed of diffusion through air?
- If the teacher puts some perfume into the dish, who would smell it first?
- How long would it take for the smell to reach the back of the room? Make a prediction.

Diffusion also happens in liquids. Tea is normally stirred to help the sugar dissolve quickly. Even if it is just left, the sugar will eventually dissolve on its own. The dissolved sugar particles will then diffuse through the tea. This diffusion takes a long time, as the particles in a liquid are moving more slowly than in a gas. There is also less space between the water particles for the sugar particles to move through. Diffusion in liquids may take several days.

1 What is diffusion?
2 Which is quicker, diffusion in liquids or gases? Explain why.

Diffusion also takes place when you make the tea. In boiling water, some of the tea from the tea bag starts to dissolve. The soluble tea particles dissolve and diffuse through the tea bag into the water. The tea leaves are too big to get through the gaps in the paper, so they stay inside the tea bag.

3 How can you tell that something from the tea leaves has dissolved in the water?

4 How do you know that tea leaves don't dissolve completely?

 How could you find out how the speed of diffusion in liquids is affected by the temperature of the liquid?
- How would you observe or measure the speed of diffusion?
- How many different temperatures should you try?
- Which would be best to use: a tea bag or a spoonful of Bovril?

A glass of fizzy drink eventually goes flat. The gas bubbles come out of the solution and mix with the air. This is another example of diffusion. To stop the gas getting out you can put it in a bottle with a tight lid. Modern 'PET' (**p**oly**e**thylene **t**erephthalate) plastics can keep the gas in. Some other plastic bottles are no good for fizzy drinks – the gas particles can diffuse through the plastic bottle, so the drink would still go flat.

5 Draw diagrams to show:
 a) a beaker of water with a spoonful of Bovril in it
 b) what the beaker would look like if you left it for 5 minutes without stirring
 c) what the beaker would look like if you stirred the Bovril into the water.

6 Which of these are examples of diffusion? Explain your answer in each case.
 a) You can smell the aroma of coffee when you open a new jar of granules.
 b) You stir your tea to get the sugar to dissolve.
 c) A breeze is blowing and you smell the cooking from a barbecue next door.
 d) A baby has a smelly nappy. You can smell it from across the room.

You should know...
- **What diffusion is.**
- **Diffusion occurs because particles in a substance are always moving.**
- **Why diffusion is faster in gases than liquids.**

What a gas!

What causes pressure in gases?

Gases are made up of particles that are moving all over the place. As they move, the particles bump into each other and they also hit the sides of the container. The force of the particles hitting the side of the container causes **pressure**. If more particles hit the side of the container, there will be more pressure.

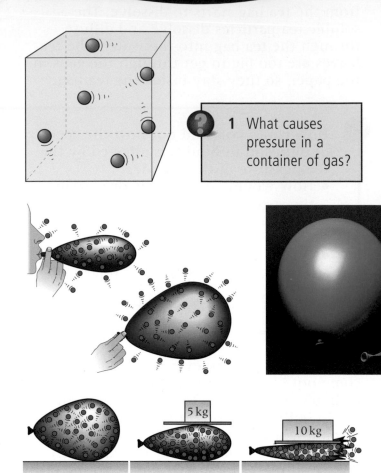

> **1** What causes pressure in a container of gas?

The air around us is made of particles, which are moving all the time. When we blow up a balloon we put more air particles inside it. The pressure inside the balloon is greater than the air pressure outside the balloon, so the rubber stretches and the balloon gets bigger. When the pressure inside the balloon is big enough to cancel out the force from the air pressure outside the balloon, the balloon stops expanding. It will only expand more if we put even more air in.

If we squash a balloon full of air, it bursts. This is because the particles inside the balloon are still trying to move all over the place, but the space for them to move in has been made smaller. More particles bump into the sides of the balloon more often, creating more pressure. The balloon is not strong enough to hold this pressure and so the balloon bursts, letting the air particles out.

A   B   C

> **2** If you make a container full of gas smaller:
> a) what happens to the number of collisions between particles and the container
> b) what happens to the gas pressure inside the container?

Car tyres are filled with air to help the car move more smoothly. The gas particles in the air are moving about quickly, hitting the sides of the tyre. If too much air is put into the tyre, the pressure of the air particles hitting the inside of the tyre can make the tyre come off the rim of the wheel. This is known as a 'blow-out' and can cause a serious road accident.

wheel rim

tyre being forced from wheel-rim

tyre tread

> **3** Why is it dangerous to put too much air into a tyre?

If it wasn't for air pressure, we could not suck up drinks through a straw.

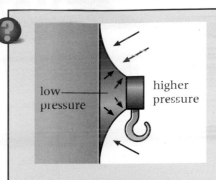

When you suck, you make the air pressure inside your mouth lower than the air pressure outside.

Air pressure from the atmosphere is pushing on the liquid in the glass.

This pressure is greater than the pressure inside your mouth, and it pushes the drink up the straw.

4 Explain how air pressure helps you to drink through a straw.

5 Look at the picture. Why does this hook stay fixed to the wall?

If you suck all the air out of something, you get a **vacuum**. A vacuum is a space where there are no particles at all, not even air particles.

If the air is sucked out of these Magdeburg hemispheres, they are very difficult to pull apart. The pressure of the air on the outside of the hemispheres pushes them together.

P What do you think will happen if all the air is sucked out of this can? Explain your prediction using ideas about particles.

Blaise Pascal (1623–1662) was the first person to prove that a vacuum existed. Before then, everyone thought that it was impossible to have a vacuum.

6 Explain why the Magdeburg spheres stay together when there is a vacuum inside.

7 Draw a poster for a tyre company to help them to explain why you must put the correct amount of air in your tyre.

You should know...

● Gas particles are moving all the time.

● When gas particles bump into their container, they cause pressure.

Summing up

What is the difference between a solid, a liquid and a gas?

Gas
- Gases are made up of particles that are well spread out.
- Gases are easy to squash, flow very easily, do not have a fixed volume and do not have a fixed shape.
- Gases have a lower density than liquids.

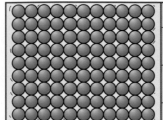

Solid
- Solids are made up of particles that are very close together.
- Solids cannot be squashed, do not flow and have a fixed volume and shape.
- Solids have a high density.

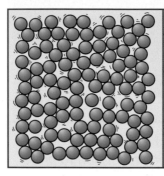

Liquid
- Liquids are made up of particles that are close together.
- Liquids cannot be squashed, flow easily, have a fixed volume but no fixed shape.
- Although they are dense, liquids often have a lower density than solids.

Particles in liquids and gases are moving around all the time. This movement of particles causes **diffusion**. Diffusion makes smells move around a room, and can mix up liquids even if they are not stirred.

Gas particles hitting the walls of their container cause gas pressure.

1 Use the information above to describe the differences between:
   a) a solid and a liquid
   b) a solid and a gas
   c) a gas and a liquid.

2 What do solids, liquids and gases have in common?

3 Explain why diffusion does not happen in solids.

Do solids and liquids expand?

When a solid or a liquid is heated, the particles begin to move further apart, making the material bigger. This is called **expansion**. Although the material gets bigger, there are still the same number of particles inside it, but they are more spread out.

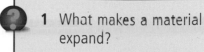

1 What makes a material expand?

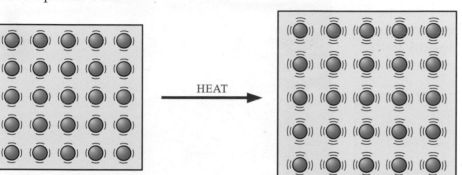

HEAT

When a material is cooled, the particles move more slowly and get closer together. This is known as **contraction**.

The expansion of solids can cause a problem for designers. When a new road bridge is built, special expansion strips are added so that the bridge can expand in the summer heat without buckling and contract in the winter without leaving a gap.

Liquids also expand when they are heated. We can use this property of liquids to measure temperature changes. A thermometer is filled with a liquid which expands when it gets warmer and contracts when it gets colder.

Most liquids contract when they get colder. Water is different and expands when it cools below 4 °C. This is why glass bottles which are full of water should never be put into a freezer.

expansion joint

2 Explain how a thermometer works.

3 This railway line has been laid with a special expansion joint in it. Was this photograph taken on a hot or a cold day? What evidence in the photograph gives you the answer?

What happens when something dissolves?

If lots of different things are jumbled up together, we have a **mixture**.

Sea water is a mixture. It is mostly water, but it has many different chemicals in it, including salt. The salt is useful and can be separated from the sea water. The sea water also carries rubbish, seaweed and sand with it. These can all be separated from the water.

1 What is a mixture?

2 Make a list of the different things in the mixture in the photograph.

Seaweed and sand can be separated from sea water by **filtering**. The seaweed and sand are trapped in the filter paper, and the water runs through the paper.

A tea bag is another example of filtering in action.

3 How does a filter work?

Filtering will not separate the salt from the sea water, because the salt has **dissolved** in the water. When salt is stirred into water the salt grains seem to disappear. They completely split up and mix in with the water. A substance that dissolves is said to be **soluble**.

A solid dissolved in a liquid makes a **solution**. In a solution the liquid is called the **solvent**, and the solid is called the **solute**.

You can only taste substances that dissolve in the moisture on your tongue. You cannot taste insoluble substances.

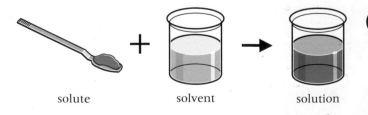

solute + solvent → solution

4 Write down the name of:
   a) two solids that dissolve in water
   b) a solid that does not dissolve in water.

5 In a cup of instant coffee:
   a) what is the solvent
   b) what is the solute?

beaker 1   beaker 2   beaker 3

Beaker 1 contains a solution. There is a solid dissolved in the water. A solution is always **transparent** (see-through) even if it has a colour.

Beaker 2 contains milk. Milk contains water with some fat. The fat has not completely dissolved in the water. We know this because the liquid is cloudy.

Beaker 3 contains flour and water. Stirring it makes the liquid go cloudy but soon all the grains of flour sink to the bottom. Flour does not dissolve in water. It is **insoluble**.

Water is not the only solvent. Nail varnish does not dissolve in water, but it does dissolve in a liquid called propanone, which is in nail varnish remover. Some paints can be washed off with water, but gloss paint cannot. A solvent called white spirit is used to remove gloss paint. Gloss paint is soluble in white spirit but not in water.

6 How can you tell if:
a) a solid has dissolved
b) a solid has not dissolved?

7 Write down what these words mean:
a) dissolve   b) solvent
c) soluble   d) solute.

8 In the beakers in the photograph, which ones contain a liquid that is:
a) transparent
b) coloured
c) colourless?

 You can't always get clean water from a tap. Survival experts have to make their own clean water.

Design a piece of equipment which you could use to make clean (colourless) water in the countryside.

You should know…

- Soluble solids dissolve in water to make a solution.

- A solution contains a solute (solid) and a solvent (liquid).

- Solids that do not dissolve are insoluble.

- Filtering can be used to separate insoluble particles from the liquid that they are in.

How can we get salt from water?

Most water isn't just water. Water dissolves chemicals from rocks as it flows over them and these dissolved chemicals give the water its taste. Different rocks contain different chemicals and so the taste of the water depends on where it comes from.

 1 Why do different samples of water have different tastes?

We can show that the water contains these chemicals by heating the water. The water will **evaporate** and leave behind the chemicals which were dissolved in it. If we evaporate different water samples, we will get different amounts of these chemicals.

The chemicals which are left behind are called **salts**. Our bodies need salts to stay healthy. We can get lots of salt from sea water if we let the heat of the Sun evaporate the water for us. The main salt in sea water is **common salt**, often just called 'salt'.

Collecting salt made from the evaporation of sea water in Africa. This is called the salt-bed method.

 2 How does the Sun help us to get salt?

In Cheshire, England, salt is found in thick layers underground. This salt can be mined leaving large caverns. The salt can also be removed by pumping water into the ground. This water dissolves the salt, making salt solution or **brine**. The brine is then pumped back to the surface and heated to evaporate the water.

 How could you get the salt from a mixture of rock and salt, using the apparatus in your laboratory?

 Salts are important for a healthy diet and for preserving food. Roman soldiers used to receive common salt as part of their pay. Our word 'salary' comes from 'sal' – the latin word for salt.

 3 Write a sentence to explain how we can get the salt out of brine.

4 Why do you think the sea tastes salty? Where has the salt come from? How did it get there?

5 Imagine that you work for a company which makes salt by evaporating sea water using the salt-bed method. Describe your job and give details of the difficulties of getting salt in this way.

You should know...

● Most water has small amounts of salts dissolved in it.

● If you evaporate the water the salts are left behind.

What happens when a solution is made?

When you make a solution, the solute does not go away. All the solute you use stays in the solution. The total mass of a solution is always equal to the mass of solvent added to the mass of solute.

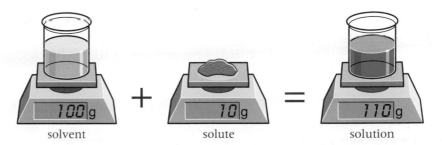

solvent   +   solute   =   solution

 1 Copy this table and fill in the missing masses.

Mass of solvent	Mass of solute	Mass of solution
50 g	2 g	
90 g		110 g
	45 g	100 g

We can explain what happens using ideas about particles.

The particles in a solid are all held together in a fixed arrangement.

When the solid dissolves, the particles come away from each other. They mix with the particles in the solvent.

The particles of the salt are too small to be trapped by the filter paper. This is why filtering cannot be used to separate a *dissolved* solid from a liquid.

solid

solvent

solution

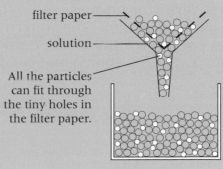

filter paper

solution

All the particles can fit through the tiny holes in the filter paper.

 2 a) How are particles held together in a solid?
   b) What happens to the particles when the solid dissolves?

3 Why can't you use a filter to separate salt from water?

4 Draw a particle diagram to show what happens when you filter salty water that has sand in it.

You should know…

● Mass of solvent + mass of solute = mass of solution.

● When a solid dissolves, the particles separate and mix with the solvent molecules.

● Why filtering cannot be used to separate a solvent and a solute.

How can we make pure water?

Pure water contains nothing but water. To get pure water, we must take the water out of the solution, leaving everything else behind. The first step in doing this is to heat the solution.

Steam irons often need to be filled with pure water and not tap water. This is because the salts in tap water clog the iron up.

 1 What is pure water?

When salty water is heated, the liquid turns into a gas called **steam** or **water vapour**. This process is called **evaporation**. The salt particles do not evaporate and are left behind. If the steam is collected and cooled, it turns back into a liquid. This is called **condensing**. The condensed water will be pure because the salt particles are no longer mixed with it.

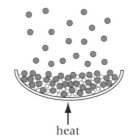

heat

The photograph and diagram below show the laboratory apparatus used to heat a solution and collect the vapour. The flask on the left-hand side contains inky water. When the flask is heated the water turns into water vapour, leaving the dissolved ink particles behind. The water vapour rises and then goes down the Liebig condenser. In here, the water vapour is cooled and condensed into a liquid.

 2 What happens to the particles in water when they evaporate?

3 a) What is condensing?
   b) Draw a diagram to show what happens to water particles when they condense.

4 What is another name for water vapour?

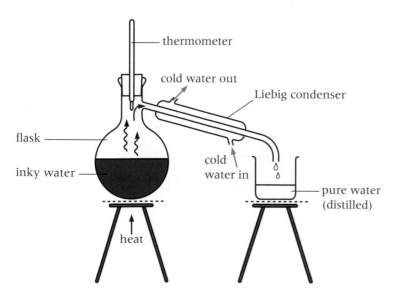

thermometer

cold water out

Liebig condenser

flask

inky water

cold water in

pure water (distilled)

heat

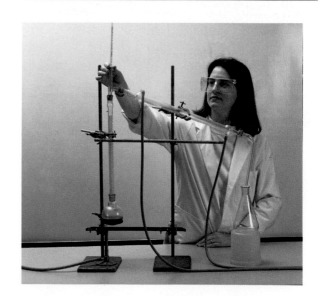

The Liebig condenser contains an inner tube down which the water vapour flows. This is surrounded by another tube which is filled with cold water flowing from a tap. The outer tube keeps the inner tube cold.

This process of separating a solvent from solutes by evaporating the solvent and then condensing it is called **distillation**. The whole set of apparatus used is called a **still**.

Stills can also use heat energy from the Sun. In 1872, Charles Wilson invented a solar-powered water still. It was a cheap way of providing clean water in poor areas of the world. The diagram on the right shows how it works.

Today solar-powered stills can be important for providing emergency clean water supplies in remote places and at sea. The still below can be floated on the sea.

 The Liebig condenser was invented by Justus von Liebig (1803–1873), a German chemist. He also invented modern fertilisers.

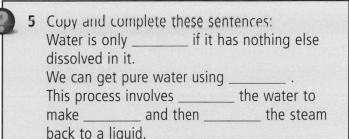
5 Copy and complete these sentences:
Water is only _____ if it has nothing else dissolved in it.
We can get pure water using _____ .
This process involves _____ the water to make _____ and then _____ the steam back to a liquid.

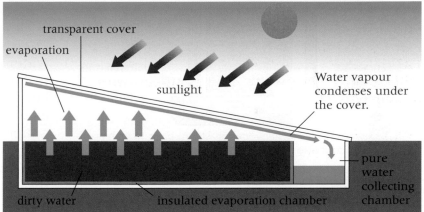

A basin solar still.

transparent cover
evaporation
sunlight
Water vapour condenses under the cover.
dirty water
insulated evaporation chamber
pure water collecting chamber

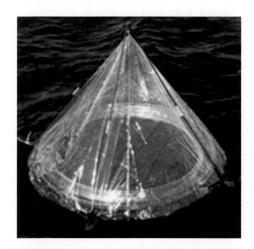

P Imagine you have been marooned on a desert island. How could you make drinking water from sea water using these items and sunlight?

6 Explain why a solar-powered water still might be useful:
a) on a boat that has broken down at sea
b) in a poor country where water contains bacteria which cause diseases.

7 Explain how a solar-powered water still works.

You should know...
● Distillation is evaporation followed by condensation.

Desalination

How can we get pure water from sea water?

Pure water is needed for drinking. Some countries do not have enough pure water and have to make more from sea water. To do this, they must remove the salt from the water. This is known as **desalination**.

 1 What is desalination?

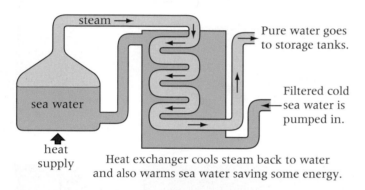

steam →

Pure water goes to storage tanks.

Filtered cold sea water is pumped in.

sea water

heat supply

Heat exchanger cools steam back to water and also warms sea water saving some energy.

The salt is usually removed from the sea water by distillation. The water is filtered to remove any insoluble particles and then boiled in a large tank. The steam rises, leaving the salt behind, and goes through a pipe into a **heat exchanger**.

The heat exchanger takes heat away from the steam and condenses it into pure water. The water can be bottled or piped to towns and cities.

 2 What does a heat exchanger do?

A desalination plant needs a lot of energy to boil large volumes of sea water. Sometimes the Sun's energy (solar power) is used to make the water boil. In other areas oil or gas is burnt to provide the heat, but this makes the water much more expensive to produce.

 Cruise ships also use desalination plants. The QEII produces over 1 million litres of water each day from sea water.

 3 When the pure water is made from sea water, another substance is left behind. What is this other substance?

4 Draw particle diagrams to show:
a) sea water
b) steam
c) pure water.

Alcohol and oil

What else can distillation be used for?

Distillation can be used to separate a mixture of liquids. For example, it is used to get alcohol from a mixture of water and alcohol during whisky production. The copper 'still' in the photograph is the apparatus which is used to do this. Although it is much bigger than laboratory apparatus, it works in the same way.

> ! *It is illegal to set up a distillery unless you have a licence and pay a fee to the government, called 'duty', for each litre of alcohol you produce.*

Crude oil is found underground, beneath layers of rock. It is a mixture of different liquids which can be separated by a type of distillation called **fractional distillation**. The crude oil is heated in a **fractionating tower**. The different substances rise to different levels in the tower, depending on how easy they are to turn into gases. The ones with the lowest boiling points are the easiest to turn into gases and get to the top of the tower. All of the substances shown here can be made from the different substances in crude oil.

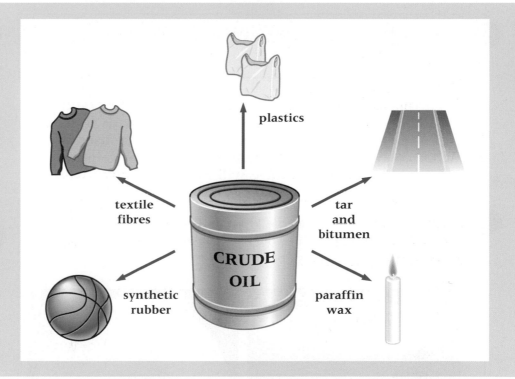

plastics

textile fibres

tar and bitumen

synthetic rubber

CRUDE OIL

paraffin wax

> **?** 1 Why is the copper still much bigger than laboratory equipment?
>
> 2 Make a list of all the things in your room which are made from one of the materials obtained from crude oil.
>
> 3 Find out which alcoholic drinks are made by distillation.

How can mixtures of dissolved solids be separated?

Orange dyes can be added to orange drinks to make them look better. To find out if dye has been added, food scientists use **chromatography** to separate all the substances in the orange drink. The dye appears as a 'blob' that is not there in real 'pure orange juice'.

 1 Four orange drinks were tested. Which one has no added dye?

Chromatography works because different chemicals contain particles of different sizes. When dissolved in a liquid, the different sized particles travel through special paper at different speeds and so they separate out.

 2 Why do different substances travel different distances in chromatography?

After chromatography, the paper can be dried. The result is called a **chromatogram** and shows a pattern made up of all the colours in a mixture. Chromatography can be used to find out what colours are mixed together in different paints and inks. Each paint or ink mixture will make a different pattern.

 3 The ink shown in the photograph is a mixture of different colours.
   a) How many different colours are mixed together in the ink?
   b) Name these colours.

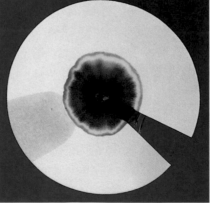

 Police have found a letter written in brown felt tip at the scene of a crime. Five people were arrested because they have the same coloured pen. How could you find out which felt tip pen was used to write the letter?
- How will you get the ink off the original paper?
- How will you compare it with inks from the other five pens?
- How will you make it a fair test?

We can use chromatography to separate mixtures of many different chemicals. It is even used by the police in their investigations.

For example, samples of blood or skin are collected from the scene of a crime. Certain chemicals in these samples are compared with those from a suspect, using chromatography. If the samples match, it proves that the suspect was at the scene of the crime.

Chromatography is also used in drug-testing athletes. A sample of an athlete's blood is taken and tested to see whether any drugs have been taken before the race. It is important to check that no-one is taking drugs that could help them to win.

A scientist comparing 'DNA fingerprints'.

The use of chromatography to identify criminals is called 'DNA fingerprinting'. It was invented in 1984 by Alec Jeffreys who is Professor of Genetics at the University of Leicester, England.

4 The picture below shows what happened when different orange squashes and food colourings were tested using chromatography.

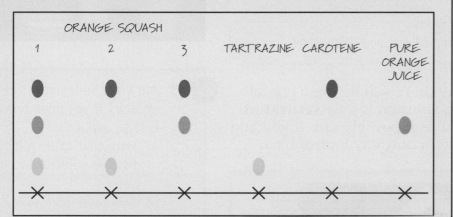

Use the picture to help you answer these questions.
Remember, if two marks are level with each other this means they are the same chemical.
a) Which food colourings are found in the three kinds of orange squash?
b) Tartrazine is thought to make some people over-active. Which orange squash would be safe to give to an over-active person? Why?
c) Why do you think Tartrazine is added to some orange squashes?

You should know...
● **What chromatography is, how it works and what it is used for.**
● **How to make a chromatogram.**

How much solute can we dissolve?

There are very few things which are totally insoluble, although the amount that dissolves might be very small.

1 Write down the names of:
   a) two substances that dissolve easily
   b) two substances that do not dissolve very well.

Even soluble solids like sugar cannot keep on dissolving forever. For example, you wouldn't expect a whole bag of sugar to dissolve in a glass of water. To find out how much of the sugar dissolves, you could add it, a little at a time, and stir. Eventually you would find that no more sugar will dissolve.

2 How could you tell that the sugar had stopped dissolving?

When no more sugar will dissolve, there will be some crystals left at the bottom of the glass. The solution is now **saturated**. It contains as much dissolved solid as it possibly can. If you add more sugar, it will sink to the bottom and stay undissolved.

3 Are these statements true or false? If you think one is false, explain why.
   a) Almost all solids will dissolve a little in water.
   b) If you add more solid to a saturated solution it will dissolve.
   c) If you add more solid to an unsaturated solution it will dissolve.

How could you find out if more salt or more sugar dissolves in water?
● What would you measure?
● How would you make it a fair test?

Even sand dissolves! Sand is made of a chemical called silica. 0.1 g of silica will dissolve in a litre of water. Sponges can extract the silica from sea water and use it to help build their bodies.

In the first beaker 34 g of solid have dissolved in 100 cm³ of water to make a saturated solution. The **solubility** of this solid is 34 g per 100 cm³ of water. The second beaker has twice as much water, so twice the mass of solid will dissolve (68 g).

The temperature also affects the amount of a solid that dissolves. More solid dissolves when the water is hotter.

 How could you show that the solubility of salt or sugar changes with temperature?
- How would you measure the solubility at different temperatures?

4 Write down two factors that affect the amount of solid needed to make a saturated solution.

5 Milk of Magnesia is an indigestion remedy which contains magnesium oxide. How can you tell from the picture that not all of the magnesium oxide has dissolved? (*Hint:* You might need to look back at page 91).

6 Are these statements true or false? If you think one is false, explain why.
   a) If you add more liquid to a saturated solution, more of the solid will dissolve.
   b) If you stir a saturated solution, more of the solid will dissolve.
   c) If you heat a saturated solution, more of the solid will dissolve.
   d) If you pour the water into a wide, shallow dish, more solid will dissolve.

You should know...

- When no more solute can be dissolved in a solution, it is said to be saturated.

- The amount of solute that dissolves depends on the volume of solvent (e.g. water) and its temperature.

What are fossil fuels?

Everything that happens needs energy. We use energy to heat buildings and cook food, and to provide light at night. We need energy to keep cars, buses and trains moving, and our bodies need energy to keep us alive. There are many different forms of energy.

A **fuel** is something that can release heat energy. Many fuels contain a store of energy called **chemical energy**. They can be burnt to turn the chemical energy into heat energy. Burning a fuel does not make energy, it only changes energy from one form into another. Energy cannot be made or destroyed, only changed from one type into another. This is called the **law of conservation of energy**.

Electricity is *not* a fuel. Most of the electricity we use is **generated** (made) in power stations. Most power stations use energy from burning **coal**, **oil** or **natural gas** to generate the electricity. Some fuels use **nuclear energy** stored in metals like **uranium**.

*Noisy things and people produce **sound energy**. Moving objects have **kinetic** (moving) **energy**. The faster something moves, the more kinetic energy it has.*

Electrical energy can be used to provide light, sound and kinetic energy. It can also provide heat energy to cook food.

*The Sun provides us with both **heat energy** and **light energy**. Light bulbs can also provide heat and light.*

Coal

Coal is a common fuel. It was formed many millions of years ago from plants. When the plants died, they became buried in mud which stopped them from rotting away. Organisms that are trapped in mud and do not rot away completely are called **fossils**. More layers of the mud squashed down on the fossils. This squashing, together with heat from inside the Earth, turned the mud into rock and the plant fossils into coal. Coal is called a **fossil fuel**.

> **?** 1 a) What is a fuel?
>   b) Name three fuels.
>
> 2 Write down three things we use fuels for.

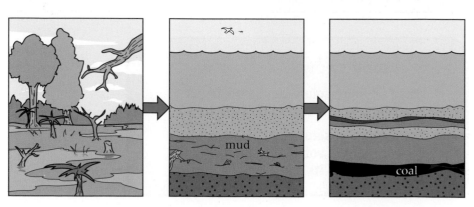

mud

coal

Oil and natural gas

Oil and natural gas are also fossil fuels. They formed from tiny animals and plants that lived in the sea millions of years ago. The animals and plants fell to the sea bed when they died and got buried in mud and sand. They formed fossils. More layers of mud and sand fell on top of the fossils and squashed them, turning them into 'crude' oil and natural gas. The oil and natural gas are often pushed upwards by underground pressure but get stuck under a layer of rock (called 'caprock') which will not let them through.

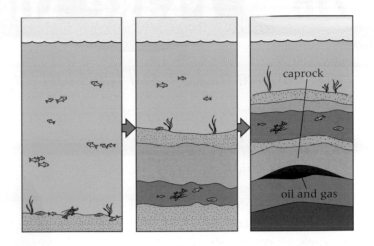

Fuels such as petrol and diesel are made from oil.

This Bunsen burner uses natural gas. When the gas burns the chemical energy stored in it is converted to heat and light energy.

Three types of fossil fuel.

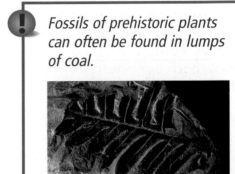

! Fossils of prehistoric plants can often be found in lumps of coal.

3 Why is coal called a fossil fuel?

4 a) Write down two similarities between the formation of coal and oil.
   b) Write down one difference.

5 Write down the names of three fossil fuels.

6 A friend of yours says, 'Electricity is a fuel'. Explain why he is wrong.

7 a) Complete this sentence: 'Energy cannot be made or destroyed, only … .'
   b) What law does this sentence describe?

P There are many types of fuel. How would you find out which fuel is best for heating water?
• How would you get your fuels to burn?
• What would you measure?
• How would you make this a fair test?
• How would you make sure your experiment was done safely?

You should know…
● The names of some different types of energy.
● What fossil fuels are and how they were made.
● The law of conservation of energy.

How can we make fossil fuels last longer?

Coal, oil and natural gas are **non-renewable** fuels, which means they cannot be replaced. It takes many millions of years for them to form and so our supplies will eventually run out.

There is only enough oil to last another 40 years but enough coal to last about 225 years (depending on how fast we use these fuels).

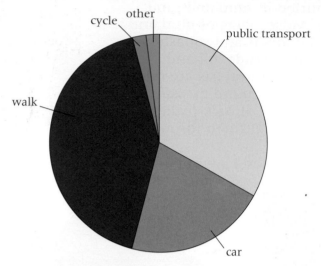

How secondary school children get to school.

> **?** **1** Write down three examples of non-renewable fuels.
>
> **2** Fossil fuels are probably being formed slowly somewhere on the Earth today, so why are fossil fuels called non-renewable fuels?

We can make the Earth's supply of fossil fuels last longer if we use less of them.

A bus uses more fuel than a car, but it can carry a lot more people. And think how many people a train can carry!

This car uses 11.9 litres of petrol to travel 100 km in town.

This car only needs 7.9 litres of petrol to travel the same distance.

nail in the last ten years.

- 62% of all journeys between one and two miles are made by car.
- It is often quicker to cycle.

* Traffic has grown up more than a half in the last ten years.

* Cycling is a good

healthier and fitter.

- 30% of car trips are not really necessary, or could easily be made by other forms of transport.
- It is often quicker to cycle to

less pollution.

◆ A rail passenger travelling by high speed train uses up around half the energy of someone travelling the same distance by car.

◆ Travelling by train is often

Cycling

- keeps you fit!
- cuts pollution!
- cuts costs!

You could save 3% a week by putting on a jumper and keeping your house 1° cooler!

It costs less to use a microwave! Cooking vegetables in the microwave takes less than half the energy it takes to boil them in a pan.

3 How can we make fossil fuel supplies last longer?

4 Write down five ways of reducing the amount of fossil fuels we use.

5 Imagine that your parents have chosen **one** of the ways of using less energy shown on this page. Write a letter to a pen friend, describing the difference it has made to your life.

You should know...

- Why fossil fuels are described as non-renewable.
- Some ways of reducing the amount of fossil fuels we use.

What other energy resources are available?

Nuclear power stations use **nuclear energy** stored in metals such as **uranium**. Uranium is dangerous because it gives off large amounts of **radiation**, which can cause cancer. However, the radiation can be used in power stations to heat water and turn it to steam. The steam is used to turn a **turbine**, which turns the **generator** that produces electricity.

Uranium was formed when the Earth was formed and so it will eventually run out. Like fossil fuels, once it has been used it cannot be replaced. It is non-renewable.

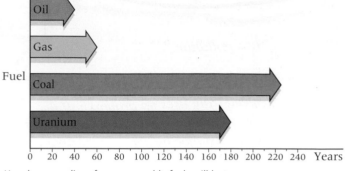
How long supplies of non-renewable fuels will last.

1 What is uranium and what is it used for?

2 How much longer will our supplies of coal, oil, natural gas and uranium last?

The Sun, wind and moving water can also be used as energy resources. These will never run out. They are **renewable**. Renewable energy resources are often called **alternative** energy resources.

Solar power uses sunlight. **Solar panels** absorb energy from the sun to heat water. The picture shows a solar power station. Solar panels heat water, making steam which can be used to generate electricity. Some houses have solar panels to make hot water for the house.

In the United Kingdom, 28% of our electricity is generated by nuclear power stations. In France, nuclear power stations generate 75% of the electricity.

Solar cells are used to turn energy from the Sun directly into electricity. These can be used to provide electricity for small towns but they take up a lot of space. Solar cells are mainly used in small electrical items like calculators.

The world's first solar power station was built in 1969 in Odeillo, France.

These solar cells provide electricity.

Wind turbines are used to generate electricity from the wind. The wind turns the large blades, and the blades turn a generator.

In some places, rocks under the ground are hot. Water can be heated by pumping it through the rocks. This is called **geothermal power**.

 Wind turbines would need to cover 370 km² to produce the same amount of energy as a nuclear power station. This is about the size of the Isle of Wight.

Flowing water can be used to generate electrical energy in a **hydroelectric** power station. Waves and tides can also be used to generate electricity.

A **biomass** fuel is one that is obtained from plants and animals and their waste. This includes straw, cow dung, sewage and even rubbish. As these things rot away, methane gas is produced. This is the same gas as natural gas.

Wood is a biomass fuel. It has been used for thousands of years for heating and cooking. It is a renewable resource because new trees can be grown to replace the ones that have been used.

3 a) What is a renewable energy resource?
   b) Why do you think this is often described as an 'alternative' energy resource?
   c) Is uranium an 'alternative' energy resource? Explain your reasoning.

4 What is the difference between solar panels and solar cells?

5 a) What do you think are the advantages of using solar power?
   b) What are the disadvantages?

 How would you show that energy can be produced from rotting biomass?

How could you use this idea to keep plants warm in a cold-frame or greenhouse?

 In Brazil, sugar cane is grown to be made into alcohol. The alcohol is mixed with petrol and used as a fuel for cars.

 6 Why do you think there are very few hydroelectric power stations in the UK?

7 Write down three examples of using water to generate electricity.

8 Choose one of the alternative energy sources mentioned on this page. Say how it works and what you think the advantages and disadvantages of it are.

You should know…

● **What non-renewable and renewable energy sources are and examples of each.**

What are the advantages and disadvantages of our energy resources?

All of our energy resources have advantages and disadvantages. The table lists some of them.

A geothermal power station.

Energy resource	Advantages	Disadvantages
Burning fossil fuels	Cheap	Non-renewable Produces gases which cause global warming and acid rain
Nuclear	Does not produce harmful gases	Expensive Non-renewable Produces dangerous radioactive substances that are difficult to get rid of
Solar	Clean Renewable	No electricity is produced if there is little Sun or at night Solar panels do not collect very much heat energy Solar cells are expensive and take up a lot of space
Hydroelectric	Clean Renewable	Reservoirs take up huge amounts of space and destroy countryside Only works in wet mountain regions
Wind	Clean Renewable	Electricity is not produced if there is no wind Wind turbines are noisy and many of them are needed to make useful amounts of electricity. Some people think that they spoil the countryside
Geothermal	Clean Cheap Renewable	Only possible in certain parts of the world where hot rocks are near the surface of the Earth
Wave	Clean Renewable	Does not produce very much electricity Will not work in calm waters
Tidal	Clean Renewable	Only works on rivers with big tides
Biomass	Renewable	Burning produces gases that cause global warming

1 Which of the renewable energy resources would be best to use in your area? Explain why.

2 Which of the renewable energy resources would be useless in your area? Explain why.

3 It costs a lot to build nuclear or hydroelectric power stations. Which energy resources would be best for countries that do not have a lot of money?

4 Find out about global warming and acid rain. How does producing electricity by burning things help to cause these problems?

Using the Sun

How can we use energy from the Sun?

Solar cells can be used to convert light energy into electrical energy, but they are expensive. Solar panels are a much cheaper way of using energy from the Sun. Solar panels absorb heat energy from the Sun to heat water.

These houses have solar panels, which help to heat the water that is used for washing and for heating. Even on a cloudy day, the water in the panels will absorb some heat. The water may not quite get hot enough to heat the house, but less fuel will be needed to bring it up to the right temperature.

Solar panels.

In countries around the Mediterranean Sea, most houses have solar panels on their roofs.

P What is the best design for a solar panel? You could use a tray of water to help you to find out. You will need a lid to stop the water evaporating.
- Does it matter what shape the panel is?
- What should you use to cover the water?
- Does it matter what colour the cover is?

? 1 What are solar panels on house roofs used for?

2 How do solar panels help us to use less fossil fuels?

3 People in countries around the Mediterranean Sea are much more likely to use solar panels than people in the UK. Why do you think this is so?

4 Design a poster to persuade people to buy a solar panel to help them heat their water. Your poster should explain how the panel works.

How much energy do our bodies need?

Humans and other animals need energy to live. We need energy to help us to grow and repair our bodies, and to move and keep warm. Our bodies get energy from chemical energy stored in food.

We need to eat the right amount of food to give us the energy we need. If we do not eat enough, we will get thinner and may become ill. If we eat too much, our bodies store the extra energy as fat. If you have too much fat on your body, this can make you less healthy.

 1 a) What happens if we do not get enough energy from food?
   b) What happens if we eat too much?

The unit for measuring energy is the **joule** (**J**). The amount of energy needed to lift an apple from the floor onto a table is about 1 J. Most foods contain a lot more energy than this, so we usually measure the energy in foods using **kilojoules** (**kJ**). 1 kJ = 1000 J.

NUTRITION
Dry Pasta
A 100 g serving of pasta has a mass of approx. 320 g when cooked.

TYPICAL COMPOSITION	A 100g serving provides
Energy	1463 kJ/345 kcal
Protein	13.2 g
Carbohydrate	68.5 g
of which sugars	2.0 g
Fat	2.0 g
of which saturates	0.4 g
Fibre	2.9 g
Sodium	trace

Food labels show how much energy is stored in the food. Different foods contain different amounts of energy.

 2 Copy and complete these sentences:
The units for measuring energy are _____ .
One kilojoule equals _____ joules.

Mars Bar Nutrition information	Per 100g	Per bar
Energy	2004 kJ/477 kcal	1303 kJ/310 kcal
Protein	4.5 g	2.9 g
Carbohydrate	73.6 g	47.8 g
Fat	18.3 g	11.9 g

 3 a) How much energy does 100 g of dry pasta contain?
   b) How much energy would 320 g of cooked pasta contain?
   c) How much energy is there in 100 g of a Mars Bar?

Different people need different amounts of energy. Your body needs energy to help it to grow. Bigger bodies need more energy to keep them going. If you get a lot of exercise, you need more energy than if you spend most of your time watching television.

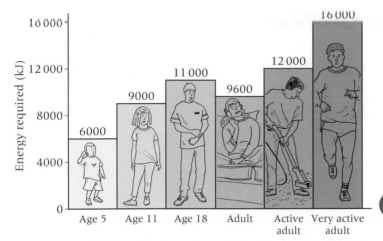

Mountaineers need to take their food with them when they climb mountains. They need to take food that will give them about 19 000 kJ per day.

 The old unit for measuring energy was the calorie. 1 calorie is about 4.2 joules.

 The unit for measuring energy is named after James Joule (1818–1889) who was from Salford, England. Although he was a brewer he did a lot of work on how energy was changed from one form to another and how it was never destroyed.

 4 a) Why does a teenager need more energy than a 5 year old child?
   b) Why do you think a pregnant woman needs more energy from food than one who is not pregnant?

5 a) Write down these people in order of the energy they need, starting with the one who needs the least energy: baby, fireman, secretary, 11 year old child
   b) Explain your answer to part a).

6 a) If a 5 year old only ate pasta, how much would he have to eat each day to get the energy he needs?
   b) If he only ate Mars Bars, how many would he have to eat each day?

 How could you investigate how much chemical energy is stored in different foods?
● How would you measure the energy?
● How could you make your experiment fair?
● What safety rules would you follow?

You should know...

● Our bodies need energy, which we get from food.
● The units for measuring energy are joules (J) or kilojoules (kJ). 1 kJ = 1000 J.

Where does the energy originally come from?

Nearly all the energy we use originally came from the Sun. Heat and light from the Sun provide us with energy directly.

Sunlight also provides the energy for plants to grow. Light energy from the Sun is used to power **photosynthesis** in plants. This process changes carbon dioxide and water into sugar.

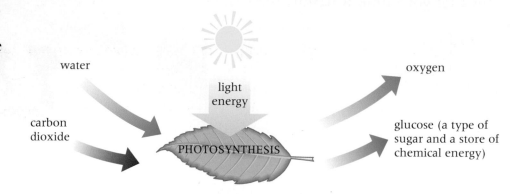

water

carbon dioxide

light energy

PHOTOSYNTHESIS

oxygen

glucose (a type of sugar and a store of chemical energy)

1 Where do plants get their energy from?

2 Where do animals get their energy from?

The Sun keeps the Earth warm. In recent years people have been adding more carbon dioxide and other gases to the atmosphere. These are keeping some of the Sun's heat in and causing the Earth to warm up more than it should. This is known as the greenhouse effect, or global warming.

Coal, oil and natural gas were formed from the remains of dead plants and animals. The energy in these fuels came from the bodies of the plants and animals. The animals got their energy from the plants that they ate, and the plants got their energy from the Sun.

People in remote places use solar power for heating water and for making electricity. It is usually difficult to get electrical cables to these places. It is much easier and cheaper to use solar power instead.

This television uses solar power.

3 What is solar power used for?

4 a) What are the advantages of using solar power?
   b) What are the disadvantages?

5 Bunsen burners use chemical energy stored in natural gas. Explain where this energy came from originally, and how it came to be stored in the gas.

Solar power uses sunlight directly, but other energy resources also rely on the Sun. Wind is caused by the Sun heating up the Earth. This is most easily seen at the coast. Air above the land is heated up quickly. It rises and is replaced by colder air from the sea. This makes a wind called a **convection current**. The wind can turn wind turbines, and also makes the waves used in wave power.

Energy from the Sun can be used to power an aeroplane.
Energy from the wind can be used to generate electricity on boats.

Clouds form from water evaporated by the heat of the Sun. Eventually the water falls back to Earth as rain. **Hydroelectric** power therefore depends on the Sun.

Only three energy resources do not rely on the Sun. **Nuclear** power uses the nuclear energy stored in uranium, a metal found inside the Earth. **Tidal** power uses tides, caused by the gravity of the Moon. **Geothermal** power uses the heat from underground rocks.

6 Explain why wave power depends on the Sun.

7 Explain why hydroelectric power stations are not very useful in a drought.

8 If you eat a bowl of cornflakes with milk for breakfast, the energy in it originally came from the Sun. Describe, without using a diagram, how the energy got into your breakfast.

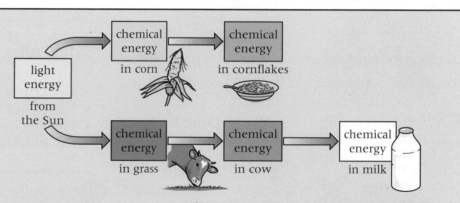

9 Unmuddle the names of these energy resources:
   i) A GERM HOTEL
   ii) AN ULCER
   iii) TRICYCLE HORDE
   For each one, say:
   a) whether it depends on the Sun
   b) whether it is renewable or non-renewable.

10 What sort of energy is stored inside uranium?

11 Design a poster to show the many ways that the Sun helps us to produce electricity.

You should know...
● **The Sun is the original source of energy for most of our energy resources.**
● **The energy resources used in geothermal, tidal and nuclear power are the only ones that do not depend on the Sun.**

How can we use electricity safely?

Electricity is very useful, but it can also be very dangerous if it is not used properly.

Electricity experiments at school are safe because we use **cells** or **power packs** that provide a **low voltage**.

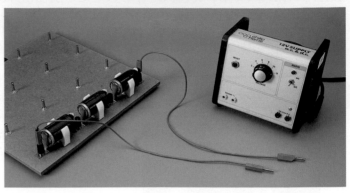
Several cells used together are called a battery.

These appliances all use mains electricity.

Lights use **mains** electricity, and so do things like cookers and televisions. Mains electricity has a higher voltage than cells, and can be dangerous.

General safety rules

 1 Write down five things at home that use cells.

2 Write down five things at home that use mains electricity.

- Never touch the bare metal parts of plugs.
- Never poke things into sockets.

- Keep electricity away from water.

- Do not plug too many things into one socket.
- Never use something that has a damaged wire.

Safety rules in science lessons

- Show your circuits to your teacher before switching them on.
- Never try to invent your own circuit.
- If you change your circuit, always switch the electricity off first.

 3 Write down five things you should remember to stay safe when using electricity at home.

4 Design a poster to remind people how to use electricity safely at school.

You should know...

- **The rules for using electricity safely at home and at school.**

What is an electric circuit?

Anything that uses electricity has to have:
• something to make the electricity flow (e.g. a cell)
• a complete **circuit** for the electricity to flow around.

The moving electricity is called an **electric current**.

Small things like personal stereos or torches do not need much energy, and cells can be used to make the electricity flow. Larger appliances, like kettles, need to be plugged into the mains supply (where a far off power station has generated the electricity).

A circuit is a complete loop that an electric current can flow around. If there is a gap in the circuit the current cannot flow.

 1 Write down two things that you need to make something work using electricity.

 Stephen Gray (1666–1736), a British chemist, was the first person to discover that electricity can flow through wires. He carried out his experiment in 1729.

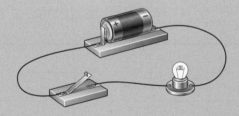

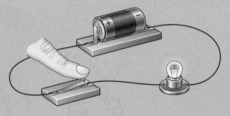

We can control electricity using a **switch**. This switch is open so there is a gap in the circuit and the current cannot flow.

When we close the switch there is a complete circuit for the current to flow around and the bulb lights up.

Not all materials can be used to build a circuit. An electric current can only flow through some materials, called **electrical conductors**. **Metals** are good electrical conductors. Materials which do not conduct electricity are called **electrical insulators**. Plastic, wood and air are all good insulators. A good insulator is a poor conductor.

 2 Why are electrical wires made of metal?

3 Why are electrical wires usually covered in plastic?

You should know...
● What an electric circuit is.
● Circuits can be controlled using switches.
● Metals conduct electricity.
● Plastic, wood and air are all insulators.

 How could you show that some materials conduct electricity and some do not?
• What apparatus and materials would you need?

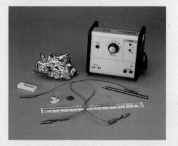

How do we draw electric circuits?

We use special symbols to draw electrical circuits because it is easier for people to understand the circuit. It is also easier to draw circuits with symbols.

It is much easier to draw this:

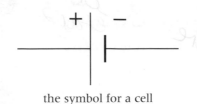

the symbol for a cell

than this:

a cell

These are some of the symbols we use when we draw electrical circuits. Things in circuits, like switches and bulbs, are called **components**.

Component		Symbol
	cell	*
	battery (two or more cells)	
	wire	
	bulb	
	switch	

* We do not always put the + and – signs on, but the long part of the symbol always represents the + end of the cell.

This circuit:

would be drawn like this:

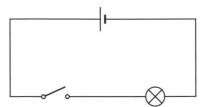

1 Why do we use circuit symbols?

2 Draw neat copies of the symbols for a bulb, a cell, a wire, and a switch.

You should know...

● **The symbols for bulbs, cells and switches.**

How do we measure electricity?

The **current** is the amount of electricity that is flowing around a circuit. A large current in a circuit makes bulbs bright. A small current gives dim bulbs.

We measure the current using an **ammeter**. The units for current are **amps** (**A**).

Different kinds of ammeter.

This is the symbol for an ammeter.

? 1 What does an ammeter measure?

2 Draw the symbol for an ammeter.

P How would you find out whether it matters where you put the ammeter in a circuit?

An ammeter is put into a circuit like this:

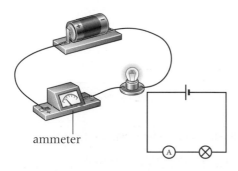

ammeter

⌛ *The unit for current is named after André-Marie Ampère (1775–1836) who was the first scientist to build a machine to measure the flow of electricity.*

? 3 a) What current would ammeter B show?

b) What current would ammeter C show?

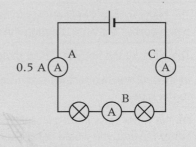

It does not matter where the ammeter goes in the circuit. The current is the same everywhere.

Current is not used up as it goes around the circuit. The bulbs light up because the current carries energy to the bulbs. The energy that the current carries is used up, not the current itself.

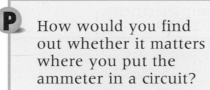

You should know...

● The size of the current is measured using an **ammeter**.

● Current is not used up as it flows around a circuit.

Go with the flow

How much current will flow around a circuit?

All materials are made of tiny particles called **atoms**, and all atoms have even smaller particles called **electrons** inside them. In some materials the electrons can move around easily. An **electric current** is a flow of electrons, and carries **electrical energy**.

1 What is an electric current?

Metals are conductors because the electrons can move around easily inside them. Electrons cannot move around inside insulating materials.

2 Why are metals conductors?

It is difficult to think about electrons, because they are too small to see, even with a very powerful microscope. We can use a **model** to help us to think about electricity.

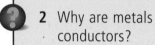
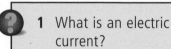

Central heating model	Electricity in a circuit
A central heating system can keep your house warm.	This circuit can provide light energy.
The boiler transfers heat energy to the water, and a pump pushes the water through the pipes.	The cell transfers energy to the electrons and pushes them through the wires.
The pipes let the hot water flow through them.	The wires are good conductors and let electrons flow through them.
In the radiator, heat energy is transferred from the hot water to the room.	In the bulb, electrical energy is transferred to the room as light and heat energy.
All the water stays in the pipes. If you measured the amount of water *flowing*, you would get the same reading at A and B. But the water at B would have less heat energy than the water at A.	All the electrons stay in the wires. If you measure the current (the amount of electricity *flowing*) you get the same reading at A and B. The current at B has less energy.

3 Why do we need to use a model to help us to think about electricity?

4 Using the model to help you, explain:
   a) why a central heating boiler is like a cell
   b) why a radiator is like a light bulb.

 A current of 1 amp means there are 6 250 000 000 000 000 000 electrons going past every second.

You can change the current in a circuit by changing the components in the circuit.

Circuit A has one bulb, and the current is 0.2 A.

If you add another bulb, the current drops to 0.1 A (circuit B).

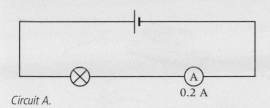

Circuit A.   0.2 A

Circuit B.   0.1 A

It is quite difficult for the current to flow through a circuit with a bulb in it. The current has to flow through a very thin piece of wire called the **filament**. If there are two bulbs in the circuit, it is even more difficult for the current to get around the circuit, so the current is smaller.

Components (including bulbs) which make it more difficult for a current to flow around a circuit have a high **resistance**. Components which do not make it difficult for the current to flow have a low resistance.

 How could you find out whether a long wire or a short wire has the highest resistance?
• What equipment would you need?

Sometimes we only need a very small current in a circuit. We can make the current smaller by using a **resistor** in the circuit. A resistor has a high resistance, and makes it harder for electricity to flow. **Variable resistors** can be adjusted to change their resistance.

The current in a circuit can also be changed by changing the **voltage**. A cell has a voltage marked on it. Cells with high voltages will produce bigger currents. You can put cells together in a circuit to get a bigger voltage.

This is the symbol for a resistor.

This is the symbol for a variable resistor.

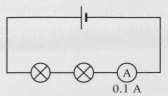 

These cells give the same voltage...   ... as this cell.
Notice how cells are connected + to −.

The chemicals inside the cell provide the voltage.

You should know...
- **Current is a flow of electrons.**
- **Current transfers energy provided by cells.**
- **Resistance is a way of saying how easy it is for current to flow through something.**

5 Look at the circuits at the top of the page.
  a) What would happen to the current if you put another bulb into circuit B?
  b) Which has the highest resistance, circuit A or circuit B? Explain your answer.

What are the differences between series and parallel circuits?

A circuit like circuit A, with all the bulbs in one loop, is called a **series** circuit.

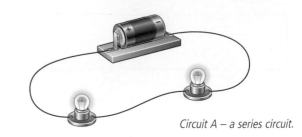

Circuit A – a series circuit.

If the bulbs are on separate branches of a circuit, it is a **parallel** circuit. A parallel circuit can have lots of branches. Each branch can have more than one **component** in it.

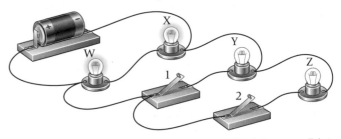

Circuit B – a parallel circuit.

 1 What is the difference between a series and a parallel circuit?

In a series circuit, all the bulbs light together. If one bulb breaks there is a gap in the circuit, so no current can flow. The other bulbs will not work (circuit C).

In a parallel circuit, the current can flow along each branch. Even if one bulb is broken, the others still work (circuit D).

Parallel circuits are useful because each light can be switched on and off separately from the others.

In circuit A, both bulbs are on all the time. In circuit B, bulbs W and X are on all the time. Bulb Y only comes on if you press switch 1. If you want all the bulbs to come on you have to press both switches.

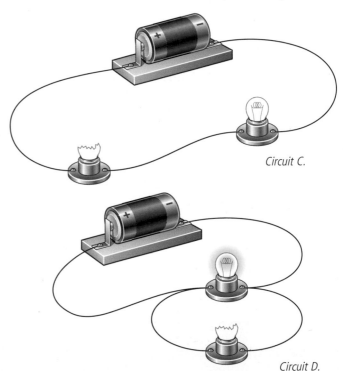

Circuit C.

Circuit D.

 P How would you investigate what happens to the brightness of bulbs if you put more of them into a series circuit?
• What happens when you add bulbs to a parallel circuit?

 2 Do you think the lights in your house are on a series or a parallel circuit? Explain your answer.

These diagrams show two different circuits
with ammeters and bulbs.

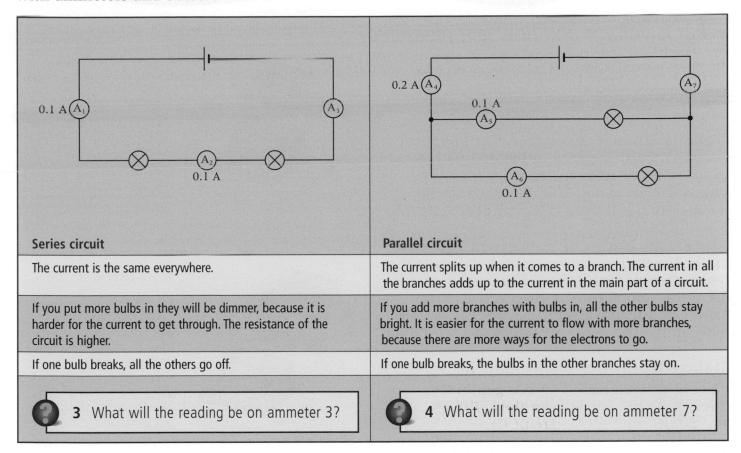

Series circuit

The current is the same everywhere.
If you put more bulbs in they will be dimmer, because it is harder for the current to get through. The resistance of the circuit is higher.
If one bulb breaks, all the others go off.

Parallel circuit

The current splits up when it comes to a branch. The current in all the branches adds up to the current in the main part of a circuit.
If you add more branches with bulbs in, all the other bulbs stay bright. It is easier for the current to flow with more branches, because there are more ways for the electrons to go.
If one bulb breaks, the bulbs in the other branches stay on.

3 What will the reading be on ammeter 3?

4 What will the reading be on ammeter 7?

5 Look carefully at this circuit:
a) Which switches have to be closed for bulb A to come on?
b) Which bulbs will come on if you press switches 1 and 3?

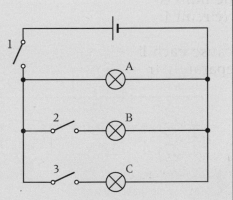

6 Mrs Jones has some Christmas tree lights, and one bulb is broken. They will not come on until she has replaced the bulb.
a) Are the lights connected in series or parallel?
b) Explain your answer.

7 Only one of Mr Patel's headlights is working on his car. Are the lights in series or parallel? Explain your answer.

8 A cell connected to two bulbs in a series circuit will last longer than if it is connected to the same two bulbs in a parallel circuit. Explain why this happens.

You should know...

● **What series and parallel circuits are.**

● **What happens to the current in a parallel circuit.**

● **How to use switches to control parts of a parallel circuit.**

Voltage in series

What is voltage and how is it measured?

A cell does two things in a circuit:

- it pushes electrons around the circuit
- it gives the electrons energy.

Cells have different voltages. The voltage is a way of measuring how much energy the cell gives to the electrons. The energy also pushes the electrons along. You can measure the voltage of a cell using a **voltmeter**, like this:

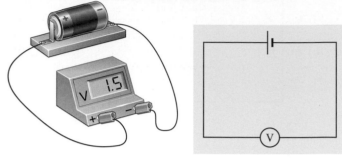

This voltmeter is measuring the voltage across the cell. The voltmeter has a very high resistance so no current flows in this circuit.

The energy carried by the current gets used up as the current flows around a circuit. The voltmeter measures the difference in energy between two parts of a circuit. It is always connected **in parallel** to part of the circuit. The units for voltage are **volts** (**V**).

If the cell or power supply has a higher voltage, more current flows around the circuit. As the current flows around the circuit, some of the energy it is carrying is **transferred** to the components in the circuit. You can compare the amount of energy used by different components by measuring the voltage across each one.

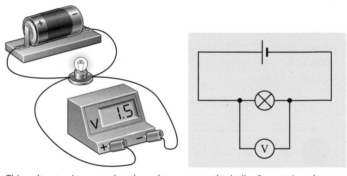

This voltmeter is measuring the voltage across the bulb. Current is only flowing through the bulb, not the voltmeter.

The bulb is using the most energy in this circuit. The motor is using the smallest amount of energy. If you add up the voltages across the components, the answer will be the same as the voltage across the cell.

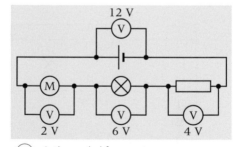

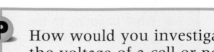
─(M)─ *is the symbol for a motor.*

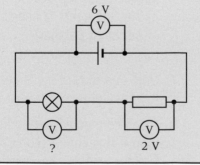

P How would you investigate the connection between the voltage of a cell or power supply and the amount of current in the circuit?

What happens to the voltage in a parallel circuit?

Voltage is a way of measuring how much energy each amp of current is carrying. When the current gets to a branch in a parallel circuit some of the current goes each way. Each amp of current is still carrying the same amount of energy as it was before it reached the join.

In circuit A the voltage across the bulb is 12 V.

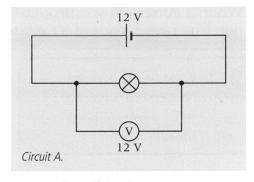

Circuit A.

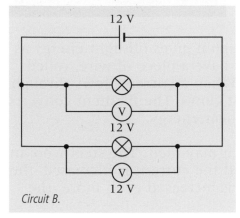

Circuit B.

In circuit B the current splits up and some goes through each branch. Since each amp of current is still carrying the same amount of energy, the voltage across each bulb is still 12 V.

Even if there is more than one component in each branch, the voltage across the *whole branch* will always be the same as the voltage of the power pack or cell.

In circuit C, there are two bulbs in the second branch, so the voltage is divided between them just as it would be for two bulbs in a series circuit. You can think of a complicated parallel circuit as lots of 'mini-circuits' joined together – each branch is a mini series circuit.

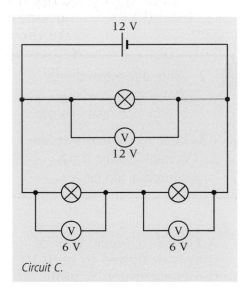

Circuit C.

1 a) How much voltage does each branch of a parallel circuit get?
  b) Why does this happen?

2 a) What will the voltage be across each of the bulbs in circuit D? (All the bulbs have the same resistance.)
  b) Which bulb or bulbs will be the brightest? Explain your answer.
  c) If you put an ammeter in each branch of the circuit, which one would give the lowest reading? Explain your answer.

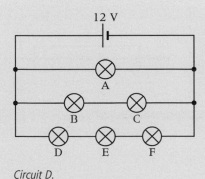

Circuit D.

How do we use electricity?

When a current flows through a wire, the wire sometimes gets hot. The heat produced by electricity can be useful.

 1 What happens to the temperature of a wire when a current flows through it?

This electric fire has a coil of wire. When an electric current flows through the coil it gets hot, and changes electrical energy to heat energy.

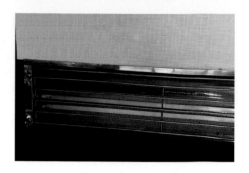

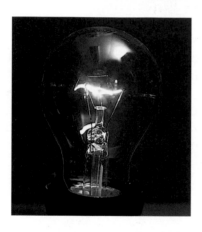

If a piece of metal gets hot enough it gives off light energy as well as heat energy. Light bulbs have a piece of wire, called the **filament**, inside the glass. When a current flows through the filament it gets so hot that it glows. The filament converts electrical energy into light and heat energy.

If a piece of metal gets too hot, it may melt. The steel wool in this circuit conducts electricity. If the current is increased, the steel wool glows. If the current is increased even more, the steel wool will melt.

 2 Write down two things that change electrical energy into heat energy.

3 How does a fuse stop the current flowing if the current is too big?

A **fuse** is a piece of wire that is designed to melt if the current gets too big. Fuses are used to make sure that people do not get electric shocks.

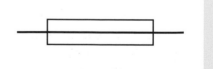

A fuse.

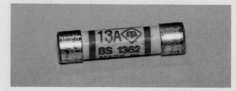

This is the symbol for a fuse.

P How would you find out how much current can flow through a piece of fuse wire before it melts?
- What apparatus would you need?
- What circuit would you use?

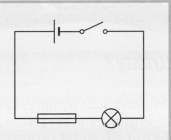

Some expensive electrical equipment can be damaged if the current flowing through it is too big. The fuse in this circuit is protecting the bulb. If the current gets too big, the fuse will melt and the current will stop flowing.

For most pieces of electrical equipment, the fuse is fitted in the plug. For instance, if something like an iron goes wrong a lot of electricity may flow through the wires. Anyone touching it could get an electric shock. The plug has a fuse in it to stop this happening. The high current makes the fuse melt, and so no more current can flow.

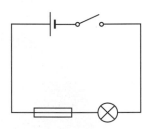

It is important to have the correct fuse fitted in a plug.

Equipment	Fuse
Kettle	13 A
Iron	13 A
TV	5 A
Music centre	5 A
Video	3 A
Central heating pump	3 A

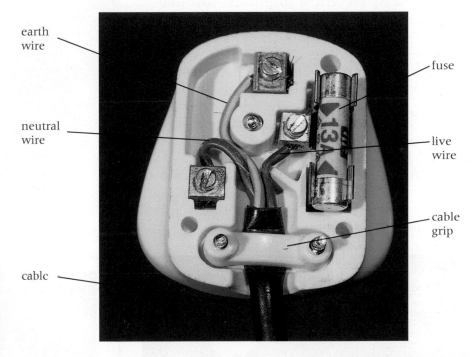

earth wire · neutral wire · cable · fuse · live wire · cable grip

Thomas Edison and Joseph Swan both invented electric light bulbs in the 1870s. They both claimed they had invented it first, but instead of arguing about it they formed a joint company to make light bulbs in 1883.

4 How can a fuse protect electrical equipment?

5 Which pieces of equipment in the table use the most current? Explain how you worked out your answer.

You should know...
- Some wires get hot when a current flows through them.
- A fuse melts if too much electricity flows through it.

How do our bodies use electricity?

When you move, your brain sends electrical signals, called **impulses**, to your muscles. These impulses travel along your **nerves**. Your nerves are not made out of metal, and electricity does not travel through them in the same way as it does through a wire.

One of the most important muscles in your body is your heart. Your heart can only pump blood properly if the different parts of it move at the right times. The heart muscle is controlled by electrical impulses, just like all the other muscles in your body.

Sometimes the impulses cannot reach all parts of the heart properly. When this happens, doctors can fit a pacemaker. A small electrical cell is put just under the skin, and a very thin wire goes into the heart. This carries impulses to the muscles at the right times.

If a patient's heart has stopped beating, it can sometimes be made to start again by passing electricity through it. The machine that does this is called a defibrillator.

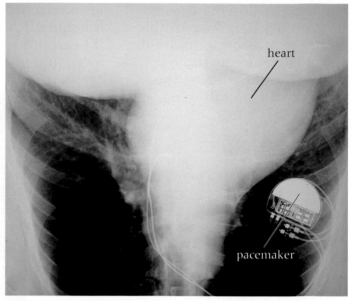

An X-ray of a person's chest. A pacemaker has been fitted.

A defibrillator being used.

Some animals can make electricity in their bodies. An electric eel can give a shock of 1000 volts.

1 a) Which cells carry electricity around your body?

b) How do these cells help the body?

Our bodies use electricity, but electricity can also harm us. An **electric shock** can burn the skin, or it can stop our nerves working properly. Electric shocks can kill people by upsetting the nerves that control their hearts, or the nerves that control their breathing.

This table shows the effects of different currents on a human body.

Current	Effect
0.001 A	this current can be felt
0.005 A	this amount of current is painful
0.010 A	this current can make muscles contract
0.015 A	you cannot control your muscles if there is this current flowing through your body
0.070 A	this current can kill you

This electric fence is used to stop horses getting into the wrong field. The horses get a small electric shock if they touch it, so they do not try to push it over.

This electrical equipment is at a very high voltage. You could be killed if you touch it.

 2 You might have a current of 0.2 A flowing in a circuit you use at school, but if you accidentally touch the bare wires you do not usually feel a shock. Why not? (*Hint:* think about the resistance of a bulb compared to the resistance of your body.)

 People sweat very slightly when they are telling lies. This makes their skin wetter and changes its resistance. Lie detectors measure the resistance of the skin, and show when someone is lying. Unfortunately these detectors are not very reliable!

 3 Describe two ways in which an electric shock could kill you.

4 How can electric shocks be useful?

5 Why is it dangerous to use electrical equipment with wet hands? Explain in as much detail as you can.

Your body has a much higher resistance than a component like a light bulb. That is why you do not usually feel anything if you accidently touch a 12 V circuit in a school experiment. However, mains electricity at 230 V will give you a nasty shock.

The resistance of your skin is much lower when it is wet, so a much higher current would flow through you. This is why it is so dangerous to use switches or other electrical equipment with wet hands. Light switches in bathrooms are fitted in the ceiling so that you cannot touch them with wet hands. You have to pull a long cord to turn the switch on or off.

You should know...
- Nerves carry electrical impulses around the body.
- Electricity can harm the body.

What can forces do?

Our life is full of **forces**. We cannot see them but we can see how they affect things. Forces can change the **shape** of something, its **speed**, or the **direction** that it is moving in.

 1 Write down three ways in which a force can affect an object.

Forces are either pushes or pulls. These pictures show some changes caused by forces.

 2 Look at the pictures above. For each picture, write down:
a) whether the force is a push or a pull
b) whether the force is changing the shape, speed or direction.

Many forces need to touch an object before they can affect it. These are called **contact forces**. For example, when you throw a ball, you need to touch the ball to put a force on it. When you go down a steep hill on a bicycle, the brakes need to touch the wheel to produce a force called **friction** to slow you down.

friction from brakes

air resistance

water resistance

upthrust

Friction happens when two things rub against each other.

The friction caused when something moves through air is called **air resistance**.

The friction caused when something moves through water is called **water resistance**.

Upthrust pushes things up. Even the chair you are sitting on gives you upthrust!

 3 Look at the three pictures showing different types of friction. For each picture write down what two things are rubbing against each other to make the friction.

Air resistance and water resistance are sometimes called **drag**.

Some forces can affect an object from a distance.
These are called **non-contact forces**.

Gravity pulls everything downwards towards the centre of the Earth.

Static electricity can attract charged things.

Magnets have **magnetism**, which attracts objects made of iron.

4 Write down the names of three contact forces.

5 Write down the names of three non-contact forces.

Sometimes there are a lot of forces acting on something. There are four forces acting on this submarine.

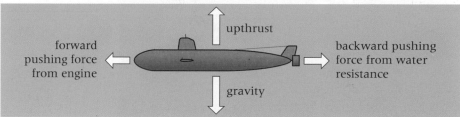

upthrust

forward pushing force from engine

backward pushing force from water resistance

gravity

We can use arrows to show forces. The direction of the arrow shows the direction of the force, and a bigger arrow shows a bigger force.

6 Draw a picture of yourself sitting in a chair. Put two labelled arrows on it to show the forces.

We measure forces using a **force meter** (also known as a **newton meter**). A force meter has a spring inside it which can be stretched. The amount of stretch in the spring depends on the size of the force. The units for measuring forces are **newtons (N)**.

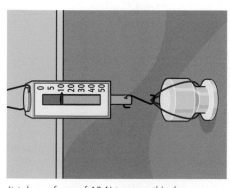

It takes a force of 10 N to open this door.

7 What do we use to measure forces?

8 What are the units for measuring forces?

9 Draw diagrams to show the forces on:
   a) a girl on a skateboard going down a hill
   b) a boy swimming.

You should know...

● Forces can change the shape, speed or direction of things.

● The names of the contact and non-contact forces.

● How to measure forces.

● Forces are measured in newtons (N).

What happens to our weight when we float?

When you are standing on the ground, gravity is pulling you down. An upwards force from the ground stops you sinking into the Earth. This upwards force is called **upthrust**.

When you float in water, you feel that you weigh less. This is because the upthrust of the water pushes up against your weight. You still have weight, but you do not feel it. An object will float when the upthrust cancels out its weight.

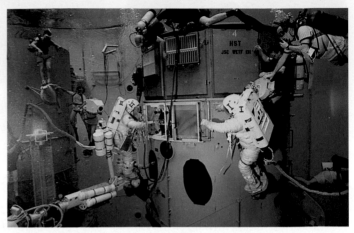

Astronauts train in a big tank of water. This gives them the same 'weightless' feeling that they will get in space.

1 a) What two forces affect you when you float?
   b) How do these two forces compare in size?

2 A boy has a body weight of 500 N. What upthrust does he need to float?

3 A hot air balloon is floating in the air. The air gives upthrust:
   a) What are the two forces acting on it?
   b) What can you say about the sizes of the two forces?

You can work out if something will float if you know its **density**.

Density measures how much mass there is in 1 cm³ of something. The density of an object is worked out by finding its mass and dividing by its volume. You can use this formula:

$$\text{density} = \frac{\text{mass}}{\text{volume}}$$

To work out density you must make sure that you have measured the mass in grams and the volume in cm³.

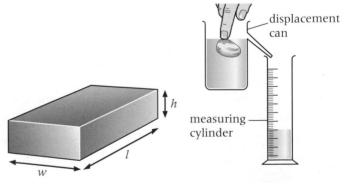

volume = *l* x *h* x *w*

The volume of water **displaced** by an object is the same as the volume of the object.

There are two ways of finding the volume of an object.

The density of water is 1 g/cm³. If something has a density less than 1 g/cm³ it will float in water.

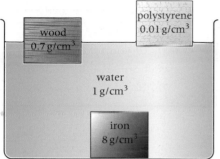

⌛ *Ideas about density were first used to catch a thief! Archimedes (287–212 BC) was an inventor who lived in Sicily. The king of Sicily had given some gold to a metal worker to be made into a crown, but he thought that the man was stealing some of the gold and mixing silver with it instead. Archimedes worked out the density of pure gold and compared it with the density of the crown. The densities were different, so he had proved that the man was cheating.*

The Dead Sea, between Israel and Jordan, is very salty and is much denser than normal sea water. People can float in it easily.

P How can you measure the upthrust when an object is put into water?
• How can you predict whether or not the object will float?
• How could you find out if the type of liquid makes a difference to the upthrust?

? 4 a) Copy and complete this table.

Material	Mass (g)	Volume (cm³)	Density (g/cm³)	Float or sink?
W	40	10		
X	50	100		
Y	80	20		
Z	200	250		

b) Which two materials could be the same? Explain your answer.

5 Why do you think that pregnant women often find it easier to exercise in a swimming pool?

6 Suggest how Archimedes might have measured the volume of the crown.

7 Steel is denser than water, so how can a steel ship float? (*Hint:* think about what is inside the ship).

You should know...
● What upthrust means.
● Which forces are balanced when something floats.
● How to calculate the density of a material.

How can you stay safe in the water?

Every year, over 500 people die in drowning accidents in the UK. Most of these accidents could be prevented if people took some simple precautions. The best precaution is to learn how to swim, and not to play near deep water. If you do play near water, or use boats, you should wear something to help you to float.

 1 Describe three situations where you might need to wear something to help you to float.

A life jacket like this is kept under every seat in passenger aeroplanes. There is a handle to pull to **inflate** (blow air into) the life jacket, and a light that comes on automatically when the life jacket is in water. You must not pull the inflation handle until you have escaped from the aeroplane.

The **buoyancy aids** these children are wearing will help them to float if they fall into the water. The buoyancy aids are filled with foam.

This girl is using arm bands and a ring to help her learn to swim. The arm bands are full of air.

2 a) Why do you think you should not inflate a life jacket inside an aeroplane?
b) Why do you think that life jackets used in aeroplanes have a light on them?

3 You would blow up arm bands yourself, but a life jacket in an aeroplane has a cylinder of gas that can quickly inflate the life jacket. Why are these two things different?

4 Buoyancy aids you wear when you go sailing do not need inflating. Why do you think airlines do not use this kind of buoyancy aid? (*Hint*: look at the photos on this page).

5 Design a leaflet to explain to young children how to stay safe near water.

Are there forces on stationary objects?

Forces can be large or small. They can work together or they can work against each other.

Two forces work against each other if they are in opposite directions. If one of the forces is stronger than the other, something will start to move. The forces are **unbalanced**.

Unbalanced forces.

If the two forces are the same size, nothing will happen. The forces are **balanced**.

Balanced forces.

1 Look at the pictures. What happens when:
a) both teams push with the same force
b) one team pushes with more force than the other?

All **stationary** (still) objects have balanced forces on them. When we show balanced forces using arrows, the arrows are both the same size, and they point in opposite directions.

If you lean on a wall, you are pushing on the wall and the wall is pushing on you. The forces are balanced.

2 Look at the drawing of the party balloon.
a) What are the two forces on the balloon?
b) Draw a sketch of the balloon, and add arrows to show the forces.

3 What are the forces on you now? Draw a sketch and add arrows to show the forces.

You should know...
● When an object is stationary, the forces on it are balanced.

How does a force meter work?

Forces can make things change shape. A big force will make something change shape more than a small force.

A spring is used in a force meter because it is **elastic**. Something that is elastic goes back to its original shape after it has been stretched. Plasticine will also stretch but it is not elastic.

The **weight** of something is the amount of force with which **gravity** is pulling it down. Weights can be measured with a **force meter**.

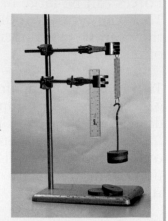

 P How could you make your own force meter?
- What elastic object will you use?
- How would you find out how much it stretches with different weights?
- How would you use it to weigh an object?

 1 Write down three things that you can change the shape of with your hands.

2 What does weight mean?

3 a) What word describes something which will go back to its original shape after being stretched?
   b) Why don't we use Plasticine in a force meter?

When you first hang something on a force meter, the forces are not balanced, so the spring begins to stretch.

As the spring stretches, it produces a bigger force.

Eventually the forces are balanced. The force meter is showing the **weight** of the object.

 Robert Hooke (1635–1703) was a famous British scientist who studied how metals behave when they stretch. His work led to the invention of the force meter. However the units for measuring forces were named after his rival and arch enemy, Isaac Newton!

You should know...
- How a force meter works.

Weighing in

What is the difference between weight and mass?

Any two objects have a force of attraction between them. This force is called **gravity**. The Earth is so big that its gravity is very strong, and pulls us all towards it.

Your **weight** is the force of gravity pulling on you. Weight is a force, and its units are **newtons (N)**. If you talk about something being 'ten kilograms' you are talking about its mass. At home, we often talk about the weight of things in grams and kilograms. This is not correct. To a scientist, **weight** and **mass** are two different things.

 1 a) What is weight?
   b) What are the units for weight?

Mass is the amount of matter which makes something up. The units for measuring mass are **grams (g)** and **kilograms (kg)**.

On Earth, gravity pulls on every kilogram with a force of 10 N. If a bag of apples has a mass of 2 kg, its weight on Earth will be 20 N (multiply 2 kg by 10). If you went to the Moon, where the gravity is not as strong, its mass would still be 2 kg but its weight would only be about 3 N. The gravity on the Moon is only $\frac{1}{6}$ as strong as it is on Earth.

 The 'true' kilogram mass is kept in a safe near Paris. All other kilogram masses are measured against this one.

 2 Why would you weigh less on the Moon than you do on the Earth?

3 What are the units for measuring mass?

4 a) What is the weight of a 3 kg frozen chicken on the Earth?
   b) What is the mass of the chicken on the Moon?
   c) What is the weight of the chicken on the Moon?

You should know...

● What the words weight and mass mean.

● What the units used for weight and mass are.

How can we control friction?

Friction is the force between two touching objects. It can slow things down or make things stand still. The friction between our clothes and a chair stops us from sliding off it. Walking would be very difficult without the friction between our feet and the floor – we would slip and slide everywhere.

Rock climbing shoes are made from special rubber that increases friction and gives a good grip.

 1 Give one example of friction making something stand still.

We can increase friction by using certain materials. Rubber produces a lot of friction which is useful to us. For example, the tyres of a Formula One racing car stop the car from sliding off the road as it speeds round a sharp bend. The rubber mat in a bath stops us from slipping.

We can reduce friction by making surfaces smooth. Skiers wax the bottom of their skis to make them very smooth. This reduces friction and allows them to ski faster.

 2 Why are playground slides made from smooth, polished metal?

Friction is not always useful. Sometimes we want things to move easily. For example, a bicycle would be very difficult to ride if there was too much friction in the axles.

This skier uses special wax to make the bottom of her skis very smooth.

Oil and grease help to reduce friction. Adding oil or grease to something is called **lubrication**. Oil and grease are good **lubricants**.

 3 a) Why should you oil the axles of a bicycle?
b) Why must you never put oil on the brake blocks of a bicycle?
c) Explain why bicycle brakes do not work very well in the rain.

axle

Friction can also wear things away. The brake pads on a bicycle eventually wear away, and so do car tyres. Parts of your clothes get thinner as friction wears them away.

New wheels for a train.

A worn out train wheel. The metal on this wheel has worn away because of friction between the wheel and the railway lines.

 4 Why do car owners have to replace their car tyres regularly?

Friction produces heat and noise. If a car engine runs without any oil in it, the large friction between the moving parts inside the engine causes it to overheat and stop working. Rusty door hinges squeak and make a door difficult to open.

Gases and liquids can also cause friction. **Air resistance** and **water resistance** are both kinds of friction.

 Young children enjoy playing on slides. Some clothes have more friction than others. How would you find out which sort of material would allow a child to go down a slide fastest?
- What will you use to measure the force of friction?
- How will you make it a fair test?

 5 How could you stop a door hinge squeaking?

6 Write down three things that friction can do to a moving object.

7 Write down two things you could do to reduce the friction between two objects.

8 Describe five ways in which friction is useful to you in your everyday life.

9 Write a description of 'The day friction disappeared'.

 One of the substances which produces the least friction is a plastic called PTFE. It has a very smooth surface. It is also used to coat non-stick pans. It was discovered by accident by Roy Plunkett in 1938. He found that some of the gases he was using in designs for refrigerators had turned into a solid.

You should know...
- When friction is useful and when it is not useful.
- How to increase friction.
- How to reduce friction by lubrication.

How can we show how fast something is moving?

Speed is a way of saying how far you travel in a certain time. This time can be a second (s), a minute (min) or an hour (h) or even longer.

To work out a speed, you have to measure a distance and a time. The units you use for speed depend on the measurements you take. For instance, if a car travels 200 miles in 4 hours, its speed would be in **miles per hour** (mph). Other units for speed that are often used are **kilometres per hour** (km/h) and **metres per second** (m/s).

1 A bus travelled 60 km in 2 hours. What units would you use for its speed?

2 You are growing a little taller each year. What units could you use to measure how fast you are growing?

Stopping distances

When a driver sees something on the road, it takes him or her a little time to realise that they need to stop and to press the brake pedal. The distance the car travels in this time is called the **thinking distance**. Once the driver has pressed the brake pedal the car starts to slow down. The distance the car travels before it stops is called the **braking distance**. The total distance the car moves is called the **stopping distance**. The faster a car is going, the longer it takes to stop.

■ thinking distance
■ braking distance

30 mph | 9 m | 14 m
total stopping distance = 23 m

70 mph | 21 m | 75 m
total stopping distance = 96 m

The distances in the diagram are based on measurements made with a family car that is working properly, with good tyres, on a dry road.

3 a) What will happen to the braking distance if the road is wet?
b) Why will this happen?
c) What should drivers do on wet roads?

There is not much friction on snow, so cars take longer to stop. If a driver tries to stop or turn too suddenly, the car may skid.

Distance/time graphs

You can show how fast someone travelled during a journey by using a **distance/time graph**. This graph shows Jenny's journey from home to school.

A steep line on a distance/time graph shows that something is moving quickly. A shallow line shows it is moving slowly. If the line is horizontal it is not moving at all.

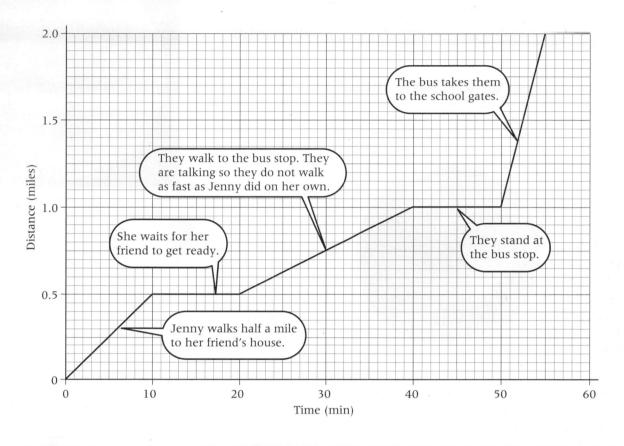

The bus takes them to the school gates.

They walk to the bus stop. They are talking so they do not walk as fast as Jenny did on her own.

She waits for her friend to get ready.

They stand at the bus stop.

Jenny walks half a mile to her friend's house.

The Earth travels around the Sun at a speed of about 30 000 metres per second (m/s).

4 a) How far is it from Jenny's house to school?
   b) How long did she wait at her friend's house?
   c) During which part of her journey was she moving the fastest?

5 For each of these changes, say if the thinking distance or the braking distance for a car will change, and whether it will get longer or shorter. Explain your answers.

   a) The driver is tired.
   b) The tyres are worn.
   c) The car is a modern sports car.

You should know...

● Different units can be used to measure speed.

● Cars take longer to stop if they are travelling faster.

● Journeys can be shown on distance/time graphs.

Why do we have days, nights and years?

We live on a planet called **Earth**. The Earth is shaped like a **sphere**. The Earth gets heat and light from the **Sun**.

Day and night

The Earth spins on its **axis**. A **day** is the time it takes for one spin. It takes 24 hours for this to happen on Earth.

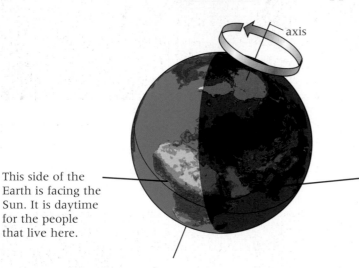

axis

This side of the Earth is facing the Sun. It is daytime for the people that live here.

It is night time on this side of the Earth because it is facing away from the Sun.

1 What provides the Earth with heat and light?

2 How long does it take the Earth to spin once round on its axis?

Warning: Never look directly at the Sun – it could damage your eyes.

The Sun seems to move across the sky during the day. It rises in the east and sets in the west. This happens because the Earth is spinning, *not* because the Sun is moving around the Earth.

Shadows move as the Earth spins.
People used to use this idea to tell the time.

A sundial can be used to tell the time.

3 Why do shadows move?

The Earth moves around the Sun. The path it takes is called its **orbit**. The length of time it takes a planet to travel once around the Sun is called a **year**.

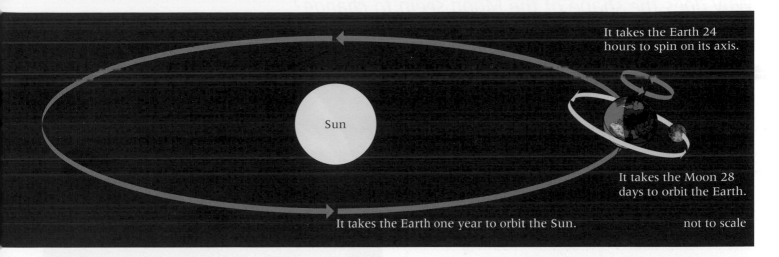

It takes the Earth 24 hours to spin on its axis.

Sun

It takes the Moon 28 days to orbit the Earth.

It takes the Earth one year to orbit the Sun.

not to scale

An Earth year is 365.25 days long. Our calendar has 365 days in every year, so every four years there is an extra day to make up the lost time. This day is added to the end of February in a **leap year**.

 4 What is a year?

5 What is a leap year?

The Moon

A **satellite** is something that goes around a planet. The Moon is a natural satellite of the Earth. It orbits (goes around) the Earth once every 28 days. This is called a **lunar month**.

 6 What is a satellite?

7 How long is an Earth day?

8 How long is an Earth year?

9 What is a lunar month?

The Moon seen from Monument Valley, USA.

You should know...

● **The Earth gets heat and light from the Sun.**

● **The Earth spins on its axis.**

● **The Earth orbits around the Sun.**

● **What day, year and leap year mean.**

● **The Moon is a natural satellite of the Earth.**

Why does the shape of the Moon seem to change?

The Moon is the Earth's only natural satellite. It has no atmosphere. This means there is no air, no wind and no rain. There is no life on the Moon.

The Moon is much smaller than the Earth. It does not produce its own light. It is a **non-luminous** object. We can only see the Moon because it reflects sunlight back towards the Earth. The Sun gives out light and so it is said to be a **luminous** object.

1 How big is the Moon compared with the Earth?

2 How are we able to see the Moon? Draw a diagram to explain your answer.

3 What would humans need to take with them to live on the Moon?

4 Is the Earth a luminous or non-luminous object? Explain your answer.

Thomas Harriott (c. 1560–1621) observed the Moon using a telescope in 1609. He made the first detailed drawings of the Moon.

The shape of the Moon seems to change as it orbits the Earth. The different shapes are called **phases of the Moon**. Half of the Moon is always lit by the Sun, but we cannot always see all of the lit part.

This is a footprint left by one of the Apollo astronauts. It will never be blown away.

Sun Moon Earth
not to scale

From the UK the Moon looks like this.

Sun Moon Earth
not to scale

From the UK the Moon looks like this.

When the Moon is between the Sun and the Earth we cannot see any of the lit part. This is called the **new moon**. When the Moon looks like a fully-lit circle it is called a **full moon**. It takes 28 days for the Moon to orbit the Earth once. It is 28 days, or one lunar month, between one full moon and the next.

Sometimes the Moon is directly between the Sun and the Earth. Some places on the Earth are in the shadow of the Moon. People standing in the shadow see a **solar eclipse**. If the Sun is completely blocked out, we see a **total eclipse**. If only part of the Sun is blocked out, we see a **partial eclipse**.

If you could stand on the Moon, the Earth would have phases.

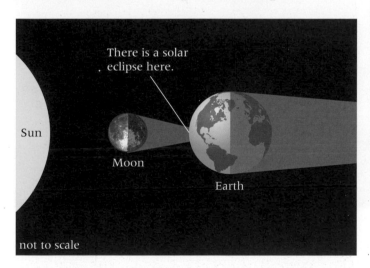

There is a solar eclipse here.

Sun

Moon

Earth

not to scale

The last total eclipse visible in the UK happened on 11 August 1999. During an eclipse scientists can study the Sun's atmosphere, which cannot normally be seen because it is not as bright as the Sun.

Sometimes the Moon moves into the shadow of the Earth. When this happens the Moon looks very dark. This is a **lunar eclipse**.

7 Would a solar eclipse happen at full moon or new moon? Explain your answer.

8 Draw a diagram to show the positions of the Earth, the Moon and the Sun when there is a lunar eclipse. Show the rays from the Sun and where the shadow is.

You should know...

● We see the Moon because it reflects sunlight.

● The shape of the Moon seems to change as it moves around the Earth.

● A solar eclipse happens when the Moon is between the Sun and the Earth.

● A lunar eclipse happens when the Earth is between the Sun and the Moon.

Why are summer and winter different?

The weather in the UK is very different at different times of the year.

These photos show the same place in summer and winter.

1 Describe the differences between summer and winter for:
   a) the length of daylight
   b) the temperature.

These changes happen because the Earth's axis is tilted.

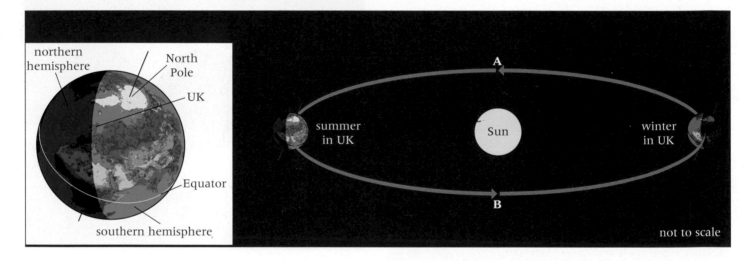

northern hemisphere • North Pole • UK • Equator • southern hemisphere • summer in UK • Sun • winter in UK • A • B • not to scale

The Earth has two halves or **hemispheres**. The UK is in the **northern hemisphere**. When the northern hemisphere is tilted towards the Sun it is summer in the UK. The Sun is high in the sky at midday, and days are longer than nights.

When the northern hemisphere is tilted away from the Sun it is winter in the UK. The Sun is not very high in the sky at midday, and nights are longer than days.

2 Explain what a hemisphere is.

3 Look at the diagram above.
   a) What season will it be in the UK when the Earth is at position A?
   b) What season will it be in the UK when the Earth is at position B?
   c) Explain your answers.

4 Look carefully at this picture. Explain why days are longer than nights in summer.

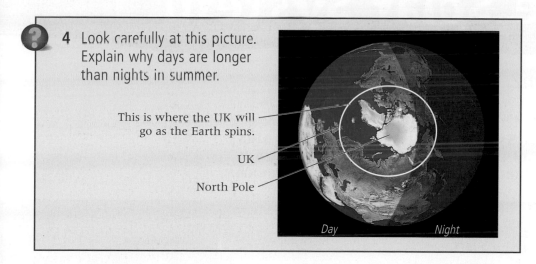

This is where the UK will go as the Earth spins.

UK

North Pole

Day   Night

The Sun feels hotter in the summer than it does in the winter. Some people think that this is because the Earth is closer to the Sun in summer, but this is not true in the northern hemisphere.

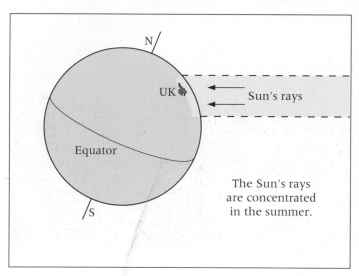

N

UK

← Sun's rays

Equator

S

The Sun's rays are concentrated in the summer.

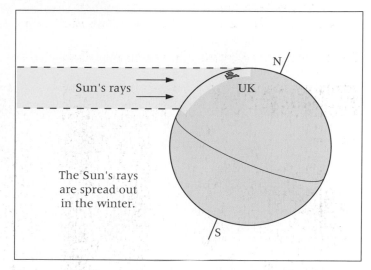

N

Sun's rays →

UK

S

The Sun's rays are spread out in the winter.

The Sun feels hotter in the summer because it is higher in the sky. The heat from the Sun is more concentrated in the summer. Summer days are also warmer than winter days because the Sun is shining for longer, and has more time to warm up the air and the ground.

5 Draw a diagram looking at the Earth from above the North Pole in winter (similar to the one at the top of this page). Use your diagram to help you to explain why nights are longer than days in winter.

6 Australia is on the opposite side of the Earth to the UK. Which season is it in Australia when it is summer in the UK?

7 If you were near the North Pole, how long would daylight last in summer? What would happen in winter?

8 If you live near the Equator the Sun always feels hotter than it does in the UK. Use a diagram to help you to explain why.

You should know...
- The differences between summer and winter.
- We have seasons because the Earth's axis is tilted.
- The northern hemisphere is tilted towards the Sun in the summer.

The Solar System

What is the solar system?

The Earth is not the only planet orbiting around the Sun. There are nine planets in the **Solar System**, and thousands of **asteroids** (small lumps of rock). Most of the planets have natural satellites (moons) orbiting around them. For example, Jupiter has 16 moons.

You can remember the order of the planets using this sentence: 'My Very Easy Method Just Sums Up Nine Planets'.

The four planets closest to the Sun are known as the **inner planets**. They are rocky planets. The other planets are the **outer planets**. Except for Pluto, the outer planets are made of gas. The Earth is the only planet that has living things on it. The other planets are too hot or too cold.

Most of the asteroids have orbits between Mars and Jupiter, but some have orbits which cross the orbit of the Earth. Many scientists think that the dinosaurs were wiped out when an asteroid hit the Earth 65 million years ago.

You can sometimes see planets in the night sky. We can see planets because they reflect light from the Sun. They do not make their own light. Planets look brighter than stars because they are much closer to the Earth.

>
> 1 Write down the names of the inner planets, starting with the one closest to the Sun.
>
> 2 Name the planets that are made of gas.
>
> 3 What is an asteroid?
>
> 4 Between which two planets are the orbits of most of the asteroids?

> 5 How can we see planets in the night sky?

A Polish astronomer called Copernicus (1473–1543) suggested that the planets went around the Sun. Until that time people thought that everything went around the Earth. In 1610 another astronomer called Galileo proved that Copernicus was correct by using one of the first telescopes. The Christian church believed that the Earth was at the centre of the Solar System, and Galileo was arrested when he wrote about his theory.

Planet	Distance from Sun (million km)	Mean surface temperature (°C)
Mercury	58	170
Venus	108	460
Earth	150	15
Mars	228	−50
Jupiter	778	−143
Saturn	1427	−195
Uranus	2870	−201
Neptune	4497	−220
Pluto	5913	−205

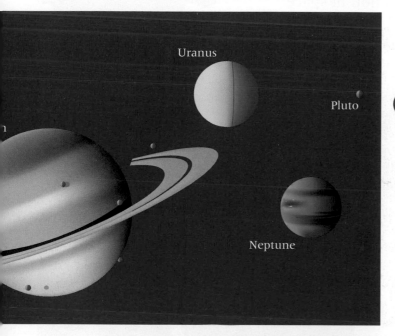

Uranus

Pluto

Neptune

 6 a) Draw a bar chart showing the mean temperature of each planet.

b) Describe the pattern you can see from your graph.

c) The asteroids are about 400 million km from the Sun. Use your graph to estimate the mean temperature on an asteroid.

d) One planet does not fit the pattern on the graph. Find out why this planet does not follow the pattern.

The Sun is enormous compared with the planets. This model in Geneva represents the Sun and the Earth to the correct scale. The model of the Earth is 4.5 cm in diameter, the model of the Sun is 4.5 m in diameter and is 450 m away.

model Sun

model Moon

model Earth

You should know...

- A solar system contains a star at the centre and other objects orbiting the star.

- A planet is a large object that orbits around a star.

- The Sun is at the centre of our Solar System, and there are nine planets.

Exploring space

How do we know what the other planets are like?

Early scientists studied the planets and stars using telescopes. However we did not get a really good idea of what the planets looked like until telescopes and cameras went into space.

Here are some of the main events in our exploration of space.

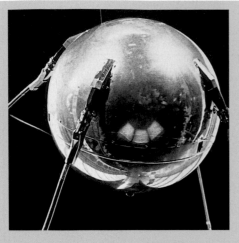

Sputnik 1.

1957 The Russians were the first people to send an object into orbit around the Earth. This was a tiny satellite called Sputnik 1. It sent a simple 'beep' signal from space that could be heard by using a radio on Earth.

1961 A Russian cosmonaut called Yuri Gagarin was the first person to travel in space. He orbited the planet in a tiny space capsule called Vostok 1. He was greeted as a hero on his return to Earth.

1969 The Americans won the race to the Moon with the Apollo 11 mission. Neil Armstrong and Buzz Aldrin were the first human beings to walk on the Moon.

1970 Venera 7 landed on the surface of Venus and sent information back to Russia. The Venera 7 capsule was the first man-made object to send information from the surface of another planet. 'Venera' means 'Venus'.

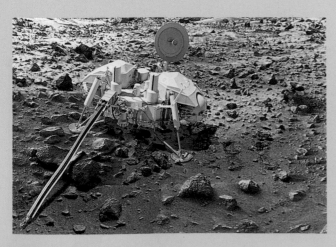

Viking 1.

1973 An unmanned **space probe** called Pioneer 10 was launched. It carries a written message in case an extra-terrestrial civilisation finds it. It is now outside the Solar System, heading for the stars.

1976 The Viking 1 space probe landed on Mars and sent back the first photograph taken on the surface of the 'Red Planet'. Viking 1 did not find any life on Mars.

1981 The first space shuttle was launched. This was the first space vehicle designed to be re-used for further trips into space.

1986 The Mir space station was launched by the Russians. This laboratory in the sky was used by scientists from many countries for more than 10 years. It allowed them to carry out experiments without being affected by gravity.

1990 The Hubble Space Telescope was launched into Earth orbit. One of the main parts of the telescope was faulty, and had to be repaired by astronauts.

1995 Instruments on the Hubble Space Telescope discovered that Europa, one of the moons of Jupiter, has oxygen in its atmosphere. Europa is the first moon ever found to have oxygen in its atmosphere.

1997 The Pathfinder space probe landed on Mars. It carried a tiny robot vehicle called 'Sojourner' which examined the surface of Mars and sent information back to Earth.

Astronauts repairing the Hubble Space Telescope.

Pathfinder and Sojourner on Mars.

1 How did people first investigate the planets?

2 What was the first object to be sent into space?

3 What is the furthest place in the Solar System that humans have visited?

4 a) Who was the first person in space?
   b) Who were the first people to walk on the Moon?

5 The Hubble telescope is in orbit around the Earth. Why would a telescope in orbit be able to take better pictures than a telescope on Earth?

6 The space probes on this page are not the only ones that have explored space. Find out about the following space probes, where they went and what they found out:
   a) Voyager 1 and 2
   b) Galileo.

What is beyond the Solar System?

When you look at the sky on a clear night you can see lots of **stars**. Stars are huge balls of gas that give out large amounts of light and heat energy. The Sun is a star. The stars you see at night do not seem very bright because they are much further away than the Sun.

The stars are all around us. We cannot see the stars during the day because the light they give out is very faint compared with the light from the Sun.

 1 What is a star?

2 Why does the Sun look much brighter than the other stars?

3 Why can't we see stars during the day?

If you look carefully at the stars you can see patterns, called **constellations**. Long ago people thought that gods lived in the sky, and named some of the patterns after gods or animals.

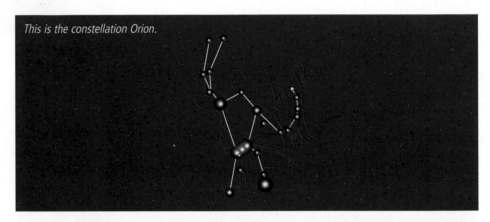
This is the constellation Orion.

 4 What is a constellation?

If you watched the stars all night, they would seem to move across the sky. This happens because the Earth is spinning on its axis as it orbits the Sun.

The distances between stars are so large that they are hard to imagine. Scientists measure these distances in **light years**. One light year is the distance travelled by light in one year. It works out as 10 000 000 000 000 000 km (ten thousand million million km).

The nearest star to the Sun is called Proxima Centauri. It is 4.22 light years away. It would take a rocket from Earth over 12 000 years to reach Proxima Centauri.

5 Does a 'light year' measure distance or time?

6 How long would it take light from the Sun to get to Proxima Centauri?

A large group of stars is called a **galaxy**. The Sun is in a galaxy called the **Milky Way**. There are millions of other galaxies, and each of these galaxies contains millions of stars. All these galaxies make up the **Universe**.

The bright band of stars is part of the Milky Way. It is the part of our galaxy that we can see from Earth.

Scientists think that our galaxy looks something like this.

Sailors used to use stars to navigate their ships. This is a sextant. It can be pointed at certain stars to find the position of a ship.

7 What is a galaxy?

8 Write these things in order, starting with the smallest and ending with the largest:

Earth   Universe   Moon   Sun
asteroid   Solar System   galaxy

9 Look at the photographs below. Why do the positions of stars appear to change when you view them from the Earth?

8 pm

10 pm

You should know...

● What a star is.

● What the words constellation, galaxy, Milky Way and Universe mean.

Glossary

Pronunciation note: A capital 'O' is said as in 'so'

abdomen (*ab-dO-men*)	Back or bottom end of an animal's main body.
acetic acid (*a-see-tic*)	The old name for ethanoic acid. It is the acid in vinegar.
acid (*ass-id*)	A substance that turns litmus red. Has a pH of less than 7.
acid rain	Rain containing sulphuric acid and nitric acid.
acne (*ack-nee*)	Spots on the skin.
adaptations (*add-app-tay-shuns*)	The features that plants and animals have to help them live in a particular place.
adapted	When something is changed to help it do a particular thing. When the features of a cell help it do its job, the cell is said to be 'adapted' to its job.
adolescence (*add-ol-less-sense*)	Time when both physical and emotional changes occur in humans.
afterbirth	When the placenta is pushed out through the vagina.
air resistance	A force that tries to slow things down that are moving through air. It is a type of friction.
alkali (*alk-al-lie*)	Substance that turns litmus blue. Has a pH of more than 7.
alternative energy resources	Another name for renewable energy resources.
ammeter	Measures how much electricity is flowing around a circuit.
amnion (*am-nee-on*)	Bag containing the amniotic fluid.
amniotic fluid (*am-nee-ot-tick*)	Liquid surrounding the growing embryo and protecting it.
amp (A)	The unit for current.
amphibian (*am-fib-ee-an*)	Vertebrate with moist skin (e.g. frog).
antacid (*ant-ass-id*)	A medicine containing an alkali used to cancel out some of the acid in the stomach to treat heartburn.
ante-natal class	A pregnant woman and the father of the baby attend this to find out more about what happens during pregnancy and childbirth.
antenna	Something sticking out of an animal's head which is used to sense things. The plural is antennae.
anther	Part of the stamen. It produces pollen grains.
antibodies	Substances produced by white blood cells that help to fight microbes which might cause diseases.
arachnid (*ar-ack-nid*)	Arthropod with four pairs of legs (e.g. spider).
arthropod (*arth-row-pod*)	Invertebrate that has jointed legs (e.g. fly, spider).
ascorbic acid	Chemical name for vitamin C.
asteroid (*ass-ter-oyd*)	A small lump of rock orbiting around the Sun.
atom	The smallest part of an element.
atomic energy	Another word for nuclear energy.
axis (*acks-iss*)	Imaginary vertical line that goes from one pole of the Earth to the other. The Earth turns around its axis.
balanced forces	When two forces are the same strength, but working in opposite directions.
biomass (*bi-O-mass*)	Any fuel that comes from plants, animals, or their wastes (e.g. wood, methane from rotting plants).
bird	Vertebrate with feathers (e.g. eagle).
boiling point	When a liquid is at its boiling point it is as hot as it can get. It is evaporating as fast as it can.
bonds	Forces holding particles together.
brain	Organ that controls what the body does.
braking distance	The distance a car travels while the brakes are trying to stop it.
breathing (*bree-thing*)	Taking in air and blowing out air.
breathing system (*bree-thing*)	Takes in oxygen and gets rid of carbon dioxide from our bodies.

brine	A solution of common salt and water.
buoyancy aid	Something that helps you float in water.
burette (*bew-rett*)	A tube with a tap at the bottom and a measuring scale on its side. Used to add a measured quantity of a liquid to another one.
cable grip	Part of a plug that holds the cable, and stops the wires being pulled out of the pins.
carbon dioxide	A gas which will put out a lighted splint and turn limewater milky.
carnivore	An animal that only eats other animals.
carpel (*car-pull*)	Female reproductive organ found in flowers. Is made of a stigma, style and ovary.
cell (*sell*) (in biology)	The basic unit which living things are made of.
cell (*sell*) (in physics)	A source of electricity with a low 'energy'. Cells push electrons round a circuit.
cell division	When a cell splits in two. Cells are made using cell division.
cell surface membrane (*sell mem-brain*)	Controls what goes into and out of a living cell.
cell sap	Substance found inside a vacuole.
cell wall	Tough wall around plant cells. Helps to support the cell.
Celsius (*sell-see-us*)	Degrees Celsius – the units for temperature (°C).
centipede (*sent-ip-eed*)	Type of arthropod with long, thin body divided into sections. One pair of legs on each body section.
cervix (*sir-vicks*)	Ring of muscle at the bottom of the uterus in females.
chemical energy	The kind of energy stored in chemicals. Food, fuels and batteries all contain chemical energy.
chemical reaction	A change where new substances are formed.
chlorophyll (*klor-O-fill*)	Green substance found inside chloroplasts.
chloroplast (*klor-O-plast*)	Green disc containing chlorophyll. Found in plant cells and used to make food by photosynthesis.
choice chamber	Equipment that allows scientists to test how environmental factors affect organisms.
chromatogram (*krow-mat-O-gram*	The dried piece of paper produced by chromatography.
chromatography (*krow-mat-og-graph-ee*)	Separating dissolved solids from one another. The solids are usually coloured.
cilia (*sillee-a*)	Small hairs on the surface of some cells.
ciliated (*sillee-ay-ted*)	Cells having cilia are 'ciliated'.
ciliated epithelial cell (*sil-lee-ay-ted eppy-theel-ee-al*)	Cell found in the lungs.
circuit (*sir-kit*)	A complete loop that electricity flows around.
circulatory system (*serk-you-late-or-ee*)	Set of organs that carry oxygen and food around the body.
circumcision (*sir-cum-siz-shun*)	Removal of the foreskin.
citric acid (*sit-rick*)	The acid in citrus fruits (like lemons or oranges).
classification (*clas-if-ik-ay-shun*)	Sorting things into groups.
coal	A fossil fuel made from the remains of plants.
combination reaction	When chemicals join to form new substances.
combustion	The scientific word for burning.
combustion reaction	A reaction in which something burns.
common salt	A chemical we use to make things taste 'salty'.
community (*com-mew-nit-ee*)	All the plants and animals that live in a habitat.

component (com-po-nent)	Something in a circuit, like a bulb, switch or motor.
compound	Substance that can be split up into simpler substances.
concentrate	We concentrate a solution by adding more of the solute to it.
condenser	A piece of apparatus that cools down gases to turn them into liquids.
condensing	A gas turning into a liquid.
conduction (con-duck-shun)	The way heat travels through solids.
conductor, electrical	See electrical conductor.
conservation of energy	See law of conservation of energy.
constellation (con-stell-ay-shun)	A pattern of stars.
consumer (con-syou-mer)	An organism that has to eat other organisms to stay alive. Animals are consumers.
contact force	A force that needs to touch an object before it can affect it (e.g. friction).
continuous variation	Differences in one feature that change gradually and have a range of values (e.g. human height).
contraction (con-track-shun)	When something is getting smaller.
contractions (con-track-shuns)	The uterus starts to push out the baby during labour.
convection (con-veck-shun)	A way that heat travels through liquids and gases.
convection current (con-veck-shun)	A flow of liquid or gas caused by part of it being heated or cooled more than the rest.
cord	Carries food, oxygen and waste between the placenta and the growing fetus.
correlation	Same as a relationship.
corrosion	When stone or metal reacts with chemicals in air or water and is worn away or changed into a different substance.
corrosive (cor-row–sive)	Substances that attack metals, stonework and skin are called corrosive.
coverslip	Thin piece of glass used to hold a specimen in place on a slide.
cross-pollination	Transfer of pollen from an anther to a stigma of a different plant.
crude oil	Oil that comes out of the ground, before it is refined.
crustacean (crust-ay-shun)	Arthropod with chalky shell and 5–7 pairs of legs (e.g. lobster).
cytoplasm (site-O-plaz-m)	Jelly inside a cell where the cell's activities happen.
daily changes	Changes in the physical environmental factors which happen during 24 hours (e.g. it gets dark at night).
data	Results of an experiment.
daughter cells	The two new cells formed in cell division.
day	24 hours, the time it takes the Earth to spin once on its axis.
deciduous tree (dess-idd-you-us)	Tree that drops its leaves in winter (e.g. oak tree).
decomposer	Something that eats dead plants.
decomposition reaction	A chemical reaction when a chemical compound splits apart.
dense	Something which is heavy for its volume.
density	The amount of mass that 1 cm^3 of a substance has. Measured in g/cm^3.
desalination (dee-sall-in-ay-shun)	Removing salt from sea water.
diffusion	When particles mix with each other without anything moving them.
digestive system (die-jest-iv)	Set of organs used to break down food in our bodies.
dilute	We dilute a solution by adding more of the solvent to it.
discontinuous variation	Differences in one feature that have only a few options (e.g. human eye colour).
displacement	The volume of water pushed out of the way by an object.
dissolving (dizz-olv-ing)	When a solid splits up and mixes with a liquid to make a solution.

distance/time graph	A graph that shows how fast something travels during a journey.
distillation (dis-till-ay-shun)	The process of separating a liquid from a solution by evaporating the liquid and then condensing it.
distribution (diss-trib-you-shun)	The places where an organism can be found in a habitat.
drag	Air resistance and water resistance are both sometimes called drag.
Earth	The planet we live on.
earth wire	The green and yellow wire in a cable or plug.
echinoderm (ek-eye-no-derm)	Invertebrate that has a body in five parts (e.g. starfish).
efficiency (ef-fish-en-see)	A way of saying how much energy something wastes.
efficient (ef-fish-ent)	Something that does not waste much energy.
egg cell	The female sex cell.
ejaculation (edge-ack-you-lay-shun)	Semen is pumped out of a man's penis into the top of the vagina during sexual intercourse.
elastic	Any substance that will return to its original shape and size after it has been stretched or squashed.
electrical conductor	A material that lets electricity flow through it easily
electric current	The flow of electricity around a circuit.
electric shock	When electricity flows through the body.
electrical energy	The kind of energy carried by electricity.
electrical insulator	A material that does not let electricity flow through it easily.
electricity	A common word for 'electrical current'.
electron	Tiny particle that flows around a circuit.
elliptical (e-lip-tick-al)	Oval shaped. The shape of a planet's orbit around the Sun.
embryo (human) (em-bree-O)	Tiny new human life which grows by cell division from a fertilised egg cell.
embryo (plant) (em-bree-O)	Tiny plant, found inside a seed, with a very small shoot and a very small root.
energy	Something that is needed to make things happen.
environment	The conditions around an organism caused by physical environmental factors.
environmental factors	Things in an environment that can change something about an organism.
environmental variation	Differences between organisms caused by environmental factors.
Equator (ee-kwate-er)	An imaginary line around the middle of the Earth.
erection	When the penis becomes stiff.
ethanoic acid (eth-an-know-ic)	The acid in vinegar.
evaporation (ev-app-or-ay-shun)	A liquid turning into a gas.
evergreen tree	Tree that keeps its leaves in winter (e.g. pine tree).
exoskeleton (ex-O-skel-e-ton)	Thick outer covering found in arthropods.
expansion (ecks-pan-shun)	When something is getting bigger.
explosives	Chemical that releases a large amount of energy very quickly.
external fertilisation	When fertilisation happens outside the bodies of the parents.
extra terrestrial (extra terr-ess-tree-al)	Something from another planet.
eyepiece lens	Part of the microscope you look down.
fertilisation (fert-ill-eyes-ay-shun)	Fusing of a male sex cell with a female sex cell.
fertilised egg cell	What is produced when a male sex cell fuses with an egg cell.
fetus (fee-tus)	After an embryo has grown all its organs it is called a fetus. This is usually after about 10 weeks.
filament (in biology)	Part of the stamen in flowers. It supports the anther.
filament (in physics)	Thin piece of wire inside a light bulb that glows when electricity is flowing through it.

filtering	Separating things that have not dissolved from a liquid. The liquid is passed through a filter to do this.
fire triangle	A triangle that shows the three things a fire must have to keep burning, i.e. fuel, oxygen and heat.
fish	Vertebrate with wet scales, fins and gills (e.g. salmon).
flow	Move.
flower	Organ containing smaller reproductive organs – carpel (female), stamen (male).
focus	Make an image clear and sharp.
focusing wheel	Wheel on a microscope that moves part of the microscope to get the image into focus.
food chain	A way of showing what eats what in a habitat.
food web	Many food chains linked together.
force	A push or a pull.
force meter	Piece of equipment, containing a spring, used to measure forces.
foreskin	A covering of skin protecting the head of the penis.
fossil	A dead organism that has been trapped in mud and whose body has not completely rotted away.
fossil fuels	Coal, oil and natural gas – all fuels that were formed from the remains of dead plants and animals.
fractional distillation	A way of separating two liquids with different boiling points (e.g. alcohol and water).
fractionating tower (*frac-shon-ay-ting*)	Large tower used to separate the different liquids in crude oil.
freezing	A liquid turning into a solid.
freezing point	The temperature at which a liquid turns into a solid.
friction	A force that tries to slow things down when two things rub against each other.
fruit	Something used to carry the seeds of flowering plants. Can be fleshy or dry.
fuel	Anything that stores energy that can be converted into heat energy – includes fossil fuels and nuclear fuel.
full moon	The phase of the Moon when it looks like a bright, full circle.
function	Something's job.
fuse (in biology)	When two sex cells join together to form a fertilised egg cell they are said to fuse.
fuse (in physics)	A piece of wire that melts if too much electricity flows through it.
galaxy	Millions of stars grouped together.
gas	See natural gas.
gas	Something that does not have a fixed shape or volume, and is easy to squash.
generate	Make electricity by turning a magnet inside coils of wire
generator	Large coil of wire with a magnet inside. When the magnet is turned, electricity is produced in the coil of wire.
geothermal power (*gee-O-therm-al*)	Making electricity using heat from hot rocks underground.
gestation period (*jess-tay-shun*)	The length of time from fertilisation to birth.
glands	The glands in the male reproductive system add a special liquid to the sperm cells to make semen. There are other sorts of glands in the body.
global warming	Another term for 'greenhouse effect'.
gram	A unit for measuring mass (g).
gravitational potential energy (*grav-it-ay-shon-al*)	The kind of energy stored by anything that can fall to the ground.
gravity	The force of attraction between any two objects. The Earth is very big and so has a large gravity pulling everything down towards it.
greenhouse effect	When the Earth warms up more than it should. It is caused by certain gases (like carbon dioxide) keeping heat in the Earth's atmosphere.

habitat	The place an organism lives in (e.g. woodland).
harmful	Another word for irritant.
head	Front or top end of an animal's body.
heart	Organ that pumps blood.
heat conductor	A material that lets heat energy flow through it easily.
heat energy	The hotter something is, the more heat energy it has.
heat exchanger	Piece of equipment used in desalination to take heat away from steam and turn it into water.
heat insulator	A material that does not let heat energy flow through it easily.
hemispheres (*hem-ee-sfears*)	The two halves of a sphere – the shape you would get if you cut a ball in half.
herbivore	An animal that only eats plants.
hibernation (*high-ber-nay-shun*)	When animals hide during the winter and go to sleep.
host	Plant or animal that a parasite lives on or feeds off.
hydrocarbon	A chemical compound containing only hydrogen and carbon.
hydrochloric acid	A common acid that is also found in your stomach.
hydroelectric power (*hi-drO-el-eck-trick*)	Making electricity by letting falling water (usually from a reservoir) turn turbines and generators.
hydrogen	A gas which is given off when metals react with acids. It burns with a squeaky pop.
image	What you see down a microscope.
implantation (*im-plant-ay-shun*)	When an embryo sinks into the soft lining of the uterus.
impulse	Electrical signal carried by a nerve cell.
indicator (*ind-ic-ay-ter*)	A dye that will change colour in acids and alkalis.
inflate	Blow up.
inherited variation	Differences between organisms passed to organisms by their parents in reproduction.
inner planets	Mercury, Venus, Earth and Mars. The inner planets are all rocky planets.
in parallel	A circuit is in parallel when the current divides, a part going through each component, then joining up to complete the circuit.
insect	Arthropod with three pairs of legs (e.g. fly).
insoluble	A solid that will not dissolve.
insulator, electrical (*ins-you-lay-ter*)	See electrical insulator.
internal fertilisation	When fertilisation happens inside the bodies of the parents.
intestine (*in-test-in*)	Small intestine is an organ used to digest and absorb food. Large intestine removes water from unwanted food.
invertebrate (*in-vert-eb-rate*)	Animal with no backbone.
irreversible change	Permanent change.
irreversible reaction	A reaction in which what you end up with cannot be turned back into what you started with.
irritant	Something that irritates the skin and eyes.
IVF	Stands for *In Vitro Fertilisation*. Using modern science to help people have babies.
joule (*jool*)	The unit for measuring energy (J).
kidneys	Organs used to clean the blood and make urine.
kilogram	A unit for measuring mass (kg). There are 1000 g in 1 kg.
kilojoule (*kill-O-jool*)	There are 1000 joules (J) in 1 kilojoule (kJ)
kinetic energy (*kin-et-ick*)	The kind of energy in moving things.
kingdom	Largest groups that living things are sorted into. The two biggest are the plant kingdom and the animal kingdom.
labour	Time when the baby is about to be born.
law of conservation of energy	The idea that energy can never be created or destroyed, only changed from one form into another.
leaf	Plant organ used to make food using photosynthesis.

leap year	A year with 366 days in it. We have a leap year every 4 years
light energy	The kind of energy given out by light bulbs, candles, etc.
light source	Something that gives out light.
light year	The distance that light travels in one year.
limewater	A chemical that goes cloudy when carbon dioxide is bubbled through it.
liquid (lick-wid)	Something with a fixed volume but no fixed shape.
litmus	A simple kind of indicator. It is red in acids and blue in alkalis.
live wire	The brown wire in a cable or plug.
liver	Organ used to make and destroy substances in our bodies.
lubricant (loo-brick-ant)	A substance (normally a liquid) used to reduce friction.
lubrication (loo-brick-ay-shun)	Adding a lubricant to something.
luminous	Gives out light.
lunar eclipse	When the Moon moves into the shadow of the Earth.
lunar month	28 days – the time it takes the Moon to orbit around the Earth once.
lungs	Organs used to take oxygen out of the air and put waste carbon dioxide into the air.
machine	Something that changes energy from one form to another.
magnetism	A force that attracts objects made out of iron.
magnification (mag-nif-ick-ay-shun)	How much bigger a drawing or an image is compared to real life.
mains electricity	Alternating current at 230 V provided to houses, shops etc.
mammal	Vertebrate with hair and produces milk (e.g. human).
mammary glands	Glands contained in the breasts of women which produce milk after childbirth.
mass	The amount of matter that something is made of. Measured in grams (g) and kilograms (kg). Your mass does not change if you go into space or to another planet.
mature	Another word for develop.
melting point	The temperature at which a solid turns into a liquid.
menopause (men-O-paws)	When the ovaries in women stop releasing egg cells.
menstrual cycle (men-strew-al)	Series of events lasting about 28 days, happening in the female reproductive system. The cycle causes ovulation and the lining of the uterus to be replaced.
menstruation (men-strew-ay-shun)	When the lining of the uterus and a little blood pass out of the vagina as part of the menstrual cycle.
microhabitat	Small areas of a habitat with certain conditions (e.g. under a log in a woodland habitat).
microscope (my-crow-scope)	Used to magnify small things.
migration (my-gray-shun)	When animals move to different areas of the world depending on the season.
Milky Way	The galaxy that our Solar System is in.
millipede (mill-ip-eed)	Arthropod with long, thin body divided into sections. Two pairs of legs on each body section.
mixture	A lot of different things jumbled up together.
model	A scientific way of thinking about how things happen.
mollusc (moll-usk)	Invertebrate that crawls on a fleshy pad (e.g. snail).
moon	A moon is a large lump of rock orbiting around a planet. The Earth is orbited by 'the Moon'.
muscle cell (muss-ell)	Cell that can change its length and so help us to move.
National Grid	System of overhead and underground cables that carry electricity around the country.
natural gas	Fossil fuel formed from the remains of dead plants and animals that lived in the sea.
natural satellite	Something orbiting a planet that is not man-made (e.g. the Moon).
navel (nave-ell)	Scar left by the cord. Often called the 'belly-button'.

nerve	Carries messages around the body.
nerve cell	Cell that carries messages around the body.
nervous system (nerve-us)	Set of organs that help to carry messages around the body.
neurone	Another name for nerve cell
neutral (in chemistry)	Substance that is not an acid or an alkali. Has a pH of 7.
neutral wire	The blue wire in a cable or plug.
neutralisation	When something is neutralised.
neutralise	When an acid is added to a base (or alkali) a neutral substance is produced
new moon	The phase of the Moon when you can hardly see it. The whole of the lit side is pointing away from the Earth.
newton	The unit of force (N).
newton meter	Another name for a force meter.
nitric acid	A common acid.
nocturnal animals (nock-tur-nal)	Animals that are active at night.
non-contact force	A force that can affect something from a distance (e.g. gravity).
non-renewable energy resource	Any energy resource that will run out and we cannot renew our supplies of it (e.g. oil).
normal distribution	The way in which the data of a continuous variation are distributed. It has a bell shape.
northern hemisphere	The half of the Earth with the North Pole in it. The UK is in the northern hemisphere.
nuclear energy	Energy stored inside the particles that things are made out of.
nuclear power	Making electricity by using the nuclear energy stored inside uranium.
nucleus (new-clee-us)	Controls what a cell does.
objective lens	Part of the microscope that is closest to what you are looking at.
observation	What you can see happening in an experiment.
offspring	New organisms produced in reproduction.
oil	Fossil fuel formed from the remains of dead plants and animals that lived in the sea.
omnivore	An animal that eats both plants and other animals.
opaque (O-pake)	Something that you cannot see through.
orbit	The path a planet takes around the Sun, or the path a moon or satellite takes around a planet
organ	A group of different tissues working together to do an important job.
organ system	Collection of organs working together to do a very important job.
organism (org-an-is-m)	A living thing.
outer planets	Jupiter, Saturn, Uranus, Neptune and Pluto. All the outer planets except Pluto are made of gas.
ovary (humans) (O-very)	Female reproductive organ. Produces egg cells.
ovary (plants) (O-very)	Part of the carpel. It contains ovules each of which contains an egg cell.
oviduct	Carries egg cells from the ovaries to the uterus in women. Fertilisation happens here.
ovulation (ov-you-lay-shun)	Release of an egg cell from an ovary in women.
ovule (ov-you'll)	Contains egg cells in plants. Is found in the ovary.
oxide	A compound that includes oxygen.
pallisade cell (pall-iss-aid)	Cell found in leaves which contains many chloroplasts.
parallel circuit	A circuit with two or more wires running next to each other.
parasite	An organism that lives in or on a host and feeds off it.
parent	An organism that has had offspring.
partial eclipse	A solar eclipse when the Moon only covers part of the Sun.
particles (part-ick-als)	The tiny pieces that everything is made out of.

permanent change	A change in which what you end up with cannot be turned back into what you started with.
pH scale	A numbered scale from 1–14 showing the strengths of acids and alkalis. Numbers below 7 are acids. Numbers above 7 are alkalis. pH 7 is neutral.
phases of the Moon	The different shapes that the Moon seems to have at different times.
photosynthesis (foto-**sinth**-e-sis)	Process that plants use to make their own food. It needs light to work. Carbon dioxide and water are used up. Food and oxygen are produced.
physical change (fizz-ick-al)	A change where no new substances are formed.
physical environmental factors	The non-living conditions in the environment of an organism (e.g. temperature, light).
placenta (plas-**en**-ta)	Attached to the uterus wall, this takes oxygen and food out of the mother's blood and puts waste materials into the mother's blood.
planet	Something that orbits a star.
plant crossing	Producing new varieties of plants by pollination between different varieties.
pollen	The male sex cell in plants.
pollen tube	Tube that grows from a pollen grain down through the stigma and style and into the ovary.
pollination (poll-in-**ay**-shun)	Transfer of pollen from an anther to a stigma.
pollinator	An animal that carries pollen between plants.
pooter	A small container connected to two tubes. Used to catch tiny animals.
potential energy (pO-**ten**-shall)	The scientific word for 'stored' energy.
power pack	A source of electricity with a low energy (low voltage).
predator	An animal that catches and eats other animals.
prediction	What you think will happen in an experiment.
pregnant	When a woman has an embryo growing inside her uterus.
premature baby	A small baby born early.
pressure (**presh**-ur)	The amount of force on a certain area. The force is caused by particles hitting that area.
prey (pray)	An animal that is caught and eaten by another animal.
producer (prod-**you**-sur)	An organism that is able to make its own food. Plants are producers.
product	New chemical formed in a chemical reaction.
property	A description of how a material behaves and what it is like. Hardness is a property of some solids.
puberty (**pew**-bert-ty)	Time when physical changes happen in the body between the ages of about 11 and 15.
pure	A substance that does not have anything else in it.
quadrat	A square frame, thrown randomly on the ground, which is used to sample plants in an area.
radiation (ray-dee-**ay**-shun)	Dangerous particles and energy given off by uranium and other radioactive materials.
reactants	Chemicals that join together to form a new substance.
relationship	A link between two things shown on a graph.
renewable energy resource	An energy resource that will never run out (e.g. solar power).
reproductive organs	Organs used in sexual reproduction. Some of them produce sex cells.
reproductive system	All the reproductive organs.
reptile	Vertebrate with dry scales (e.g. snake).
reservoir (rez-zer-vwarr)	Man-made lake.
resistance	A way of saying how difficult it is for electricity to flow through something.

resistor	A component that makes it difficult for electricity to flow – resistors are used to control the size of a current in a circuit.
reversible change	A change in which what you end up with can easily be turned back into what you started with.
room temperature	About 20 °C.
root	Plant organ used to take water out of the soil.
root hair cell	Cell found in roots. The root hair has a large surface area to help the cell absorb water quickly.
rust	Substance formed when iron or steel reacts with oxygen and water.
salts	Chemicals from rocks that have dissolved in water.
sample	A small part of something. If you sample something you take a small part of it. You use your results from the small part to suggest what the rest of it is like.
satellite	Anything that orbits a planet.
saturated	A solution that contains as much dissolved solid as it possibly can.
scavenger	Carnivore that eats animals but does not kill them itself. Animals can have died or been killed by other animals.
scrotum (scrow-tum)	Bag of skin containing the testes in males.
seasonal changes	Changes in the physical environmental factors of an environment which happen during a year (e.g. it gets colder in winter).
seed coat	Hard outer covering of a seed
seeds	Grow into new plants. Made by conifers and flowering plants.
segment	Some animals have bodies that are divided into obvious sections called segments.
self-pollination	Transfer of pollen from an anther to stigma of the same plant.
semen (see-men)	A mixture of sperm cells and fluids released by men during sexual intercourse.
series circuit	A circuit where there is only one loop of wire.
sex cell	A cell used for sexual reproduction.
sex hormones (hor-moans)	Chemicals released in our bodies that control the menstrual cycle and puberty.
sexual reproduction (re-pro-**duck**-shun)	Making new living things which involves a male and a female.
skin	Organ used for protection and feeling.
slide	Glass sheet that a specimen is put on.
solar cells	Flat plates that convert light energy into electrical energy.
solar eclipse	When the Moon is between the Sun and the Earth, and casts a shadow on part of the Earth.
solar panels	Flat plates that use the Sun's energy to heat water.
solar power	Making electricity by using light or heat energy from the Sun.
solar system	A star with planets and other objects orbiting it.
solid	Something with a fixed shape and volume.
solubility (sol-you-**bill**-ity)	The amount of a solid that will dissolve in 100 g of a liquid.
soluble (sol-you-bull)	A solid that can dissolve in a liquid. Salt is soluble in water.
solute	The solid that has dissolved in a liquid to make a solution.
solution (sol-oo-shun)	When a solid has dissolved in a liquid.
solvent	The liquid that has dissolved a solid to make a solution.
sound energy	The kind of energy made by anything that is making a noise.
space probe	An unmanned space craft that has cameras and other equipment to find out about other planets.
space station	A man-made satellite orbiting around the Earth, big enough for several astronauts to live in for months or years.
species (spee-shees)	A group of organisms that can reproduce with each other to produce offspring that will also be able to reproduce.
specimen (spess-im-men)	What you look at down a microscope.
speed	How fast something is moving. Often measured in metres per second (m/s).
sperm cell	The male sex cell in humans.

sperm count	The number of sperm cells produced by a man's testes.
sperm duct	Tube that carries sperm from the testes to the urethra.
sphere (sfear)	A shape like a ball.
stage	Part of the microscope. You put slides on it.
stain	Dye used to colour parts of a cell to make them easier to see.
stamen (stay-men)	Male reproductive organ found in flowers. It is made of an anther and a filament.
star	A large ball of gas that gives off lots of heat and light energy.
states of matter	There are three different forms in which a substance can be in; solid, liquid and gas. These are the three states of matter.
static electricity	A force which attracts things with extra electrical charges on them.
stationary	Not moving.
steam	Water as a gas. Also called water vapour.
stem	Plant organ used to take water to the leaves and to support the leaves.
stigma	Part of the carpel. It is where pollen lands.
still	The apparatus used for distillation.
stomach (stum-ack)	Organ used to help break up food.
stopping distance	The distance a car moves while it is stopping. The stopping distance is equal to the thinking distance and the braking distance added together.
strain energy	The kind of energy stored in stretched or squashed things which can bounce back to their original shapes.
style	Part of the carpel connecting the stigma to the ovary.
sulphuric acid	A common acid. Used in car batteries.
Sun	The star that the Earth orbits around.
sweepnet	A net which is swept through long grass to catch tiny animals.
sweeteners	A substance that makes things taste sweeter. Sugar is a natural sweetener.
switch	Turns electricity on or off, by closing or opening a gap in a circuit.
telescope	An instrument that helps us to see distant things like the stars or planets.
testis	Male reproductive organ in human males. Produces sperm cells. The plural is testes.
test tube baby	A baby where the fertilised egg cell was produced by IVF.
theory (thear-ree)	An idea about why things work the way they do. Scientists use their imaginations to come up with a theory.
thinking distance	The distance a car travels while the driver is deciding to press the brake pedal.
thorax	Middle section of an insect body.
tidal power	Making electricity using the moving (kinetic) energy from tides.
tissue (tiss-you)	A group of the same cells all doing the same job.
top predator	The last animal in a food chain.
total eclipse	A solar eclipse when the Moon completely blocks out light from the Sun.
transferred	When something has moved from one thing to another.
transformer	Piece of equipment used to change voltages.
transparent	Another word for see-through.
tree beating	Hitting the branches of a tree and collecting small animals that fall out.
turbine	The machine in a power station that is pushed round by water or steam and turns the generator.
umbilical cord (Um-bill-ick-al)	See 'cord'
unbalanced forces	When two forces working in opposite directions are not the same strength.
universal indicator	A mixture of indicators giving a different colour depending on how weak or strong an acid or an alkali is.
universe	All the galaxies and the space between them make up the universe.
unmanned	Something that has no humans on it.
unstable	A chemical that can decompose very easily is unstable.
upthrust	A force that pushes things up.
uranium (yer-rain-ee-um)	A fuel used in nuclear power stations.
urethra (you-ree-thra)	A tube carrying semen or urine running down the centre of the penis in males. A tube carrying urine in females.
uterus (you-ter-ous)	Organ in females in which a baby develops.
vacuole (vack-you-oll)	Storage space in plant cells.
vacuum (vack-youm)	A completely empty space.
vagina (vaj-eye-na)	Tube in females. The penis is placed here during sexual intercourse.
variable (vair-ri-able)	A factor in an experiment that can change.
variable resistor	A resistor that can be adjusted to change the amount of resistance it has.
variation	The differences between things.
variety	A plant or animal that is different in some way from its parents.
vertebrate (vert-eb-rate)	An animal with a backbone.
vibrate	Move backwards and forwards.
voltage	The amount of pushing that a cell does is called the voltage.
voltmeter	A component that measures voltage.
volts	The unit of voltage (V).
water resistance	A force that tries to slow things down that are moving through water. It is a type of friction.
water vapour (vay-per)	Water as a gas. Also called steam.
wave power	Making electricity using the waves in the sea as a source of energy.
weight	The amount of force with which gravity pulls something towards the Earth. It is measured in Newtons (N).
wind turbine	A kind of windmill that generates electricity using energy from the wind.
word equation	A way of writing out what happens in a chemical reaction.
xylem tissue	Found in roots, stems and leaves. Transports water.
xylem tube (z-eye-lem)	Hollow tube formed from xylem cells and used to carry water up a plant.
year	The length of time it takes a planet to go around the Sun. One year on Earth is 365.25 days.

Index

Pearson Education
Edinburgh Gate
Harlow
Essex CM20 2JE

ISBN: 0 582 53572 7

Design Concept by Pentacor plc, High Wycombe
Designed and produced by Gecko Ltd, Bicester, Oxon
Printed in China GCC/05

The publisher's policy is to use paper manufactured from sustainable forests.

Acknowledgements
The publisher would like to thank The Latymer School, Edmonton, and Leventhrorpe School, Sawbridgeworth, for their help in the production of this book.

We are grateful to the following for permission to reproduce photographs:

John Adds, p9; Adtranz, p137 *top left*, p137 *top right*; B & C Alexander, p30 *centre left*; Allsport UK, p128 *left* (Gary M. Prior), p129 *left* (Craig Prentis); Janette Ames, p47 *top left*, p47 *top centre*, p47 *top right*; Ardea, p19 *top right* (A. E. Bomford), p40 *above centre*, p44 *centre left*, p44 *bottom centre* and p44 *bottom left* (John Daniels); Art Directors & TRIP, p8 *bottom*, p10 *left* and p10 *centre* (M. I. Walker), p23 *right* (S Grant), p31 *top* (Helene Rogers), p36 *top right* (P. Chadwick), p37 *centre left* (B. Gadsby), p37 *below right* (M. Thornton), p39 *right* (P. Chadwick), p43 *top* Helene Rogers), p47 *bottom* (Chris Parker), p55 *top right* (Viesti Collection/M. Blanford), p71 *centre left* , p71 *centre right*, p75 *bottom left* (Helene Rogers), p96 *top*, p96 *bottom* (J. Ringland), p113 *right* (M. Feeney), p128 *right* (S. Grant), p132 *centre* (J. Wender); Elie Bernager, p44 *centre right*; Gareth Boden, p7, p15, p25, p60 *bottom*, p62, p69 *centre*, p81 *bottom right*, p84 *centre*, p84 *bottom*, p85 *top*, p85 *bottom*, p86, p90 *bottom*, p91 *top*, p91 *centre*, p94 *bottom*, p95 *right*, p98 *top*, p98 *bottom left*, p98 *bottom right*, p100 *top*, p100 *bottom*, p101 *top*, p101 *bottom*, p103 *centre*, p107 *bottom*, p134, p91 *bottom*; Robert Brons/BPS, p10 *right*; Professor W. J. Broughton, p11 *left*, p12 *bottom left*; Bubbles, p24 *top* (Dr Hercules Robinson), p27 *bottom*; p28 *top* and p28 *bottom* (Angela Hampton), p132 *right* (Jennie Woodcock), p137 *bottom* (Ian West); Bureau International Des Poid et Mesures, p135; J. Allan Cash, p16, p102 *top right*, p102 *bottom*, p144 *left*, p144 *right*; Ken Catania, p33 *centre right*; Centura Foods, p84 *top*; Trevor A. Clarke, p8 *top left*; John Cleare Mountain Camera, p111 *top*; Trevor Clifford, p37 *top*, p46, p48 *bottom right*, p57 *left*, p58 *left*, p59 *bottom*, p64 *bottom*, p68 *bottom*, p69 *bottom*, p70 *top left*, p70 *top right*, p70 *centre left*, p70 *centre right*, p70 *bottom left*, p70 *bottom right*, p71 *bottom*, p73 *bottom*, p87 *top*, p87 *bottom*, p109 *bottom*, p111 *bottom*, p114 *top*, p114 *bottom*, p115, p117 *top*, p117 *bottom*, p124 *centre left*, p124 *centre right*, p131 *bottom*; Bruce Coleman Collection, p35 *bottom right* (Allan G. Potts), p55 *top left* (Fred Bruemmer), p55 *top centre* (Joe McDonald), p55 *bottom left* (Kim Taylor), p148 *top* (Astrofoto); Corbis, p44 *bottom right* (Ann Purcell), p58 *right* (Lowell Georgia); Corbis/Stock Market/Dimaggio/Kalish, p49 *top*; Corbis/Stock Market, p66 (Firefly Productions); Äslög Dahl, p14 *right*; Dorling Kindersley, p18 *top* (Frank Greenaway), p30 *centre right* (Neil Fletcher), p32 *top left* (Steve Gorton), p33 *bottom*; p36 *top left* (Frank Greenaway), p40 *top* (Tim Ridley), p41 *top centre* (Peter Chadwick), p42 *top left*, p51 *top*; p52 *top left* (Francesca York), p52 *bottom left* (Jane Miller), p53 *top left*; p53 *top centre left* and p53 *top right* (Frank Greenaway), p53 *top centre* (Stephen Oliver), p53 *top centre right* (Geoff Dann), p53 *bottom left* (Geoff Brightling), p53 *bottom centre left*, p53 *bottom centre*, p53 *bottom centre right* (Mike Dunning), p53 *bottom right* (Geoff Dann); p54 *top*: snail, p54 *top*: earthworm (Geoff Dann), p54 *top*: jellyfish and spider (Frank Greenaway), p54 *top*: starfish (Stephen Oliver), p54 *top*: roundworm (Kim Taylor), p54 *bottom*: fly, sea urchin and snail; p54 *bottom*: brittle star and leech (Frank Greenaway), p54 *bottom*: lobster (Dave King), p54 *bottom*: crab and starfish (Stephen Oliver), p54 *bottom*: butterfly and slug (Kim Taylor), p54 *bottom*: scorpion and weevil (Jerry Young), p55 *bottom right* (inset), p104 *top* (Peter James Kindersley), p55 *bottom right* Dorling Kindersley/Natural History Museum/Harry Taylor; Ecoscene, p39 *left* (Andrew Brown), p41 *top right* (John Farmer), p59 *top* (Anthony Cooper), p110 (Angela Hampton); Mary Evans Picture Library, p8 *top right*; FLPA, p18 *bottom* (Winifried Wisniewski), p30 *top centre* (Martin H. Smith), p32 *centre* (Hugh Clark), p33 *centre right* (Minden Pictures), p37 *centre right* (Roger Wilmshurst), p42 *top right* (A. R. Hamblin), p42 *bottom right* (Eric & David Hosking); Theodore H Fleming, p34 *top*, p34 *centre*; Flight International, p132 *left*; GeoScience Features Picture Library, p103 *right*; Getty Images, p11 *right* (Spike Walker), p12 *top left* (G. W. Willis/BPS), p141 (Chad Ehlers), p17 *top* (Dave Schiefelbein), p23 *left* (Peter Cade), p27 *top* (Roger Tully), p33 *top left* (J. Szkodzinski), p35 *top*, p35 *centre*; p45 *left* (James Cotier), p73 *top* (Richard Kaylin), p76 *top left*, p76 *top centre* and *top right* (Isy-Schwart), p97 (Alan Becker), p102 *top left* (David Stewart), p106 *top* (Jamey Stillings), p126 *top* (David Job), p126 *bottom left* (Bruce Ayres), p136 *top* (Philip & Karen Smith); The Ronald Grant Archive, p47 *above centre*; Robert Harding Picture Library, p17 *above centre right* (Michael Jenner), p130 *bottom* (Fred Frieberg); Highways Agency/McKenzie Clark, p78 *top*; Home Office, p72 *bottom left*, p72 *bottom right*; Henry Iddon/Stock Shot, p136 *centre*; Penny Johnson, p88; Andrew Lambert, p68 *centre*, p71 *top left*, p89 *top*, p89 *bottom left*, p89 *below right*, p107 *top*, p124 *top left*, p125, p129 *centre*, p129 *right*, p140 *bottom*; Mark Levesley, p47 *above centre left*, p124 *bottom left*, p147; Life Science Images, p74; Metropolitan Police Service, p51 *centre*, p51 *bottom*; P. Morris, p55 *bottom centre*; Paul Mulcahy, p43 *centre*, p48 *top*, p56 *top*, p56 *centre*, p56 *bottom*, p57 *right*, p64 *centre*, p67 *top left*, p67 *top right*, p67 *bottom left*, p67 *bottom right*, p81 *bottom left*, p94 *top*, p124 *top right*, p127 *left*, p127 *right*, p136 *bottom*; NASA, p140 *top*, p142 *bottom*, p143 *top*, p148 *centre*, p149 *top*; Natural Visions/Heather Angel, p30 *top left*, p34 *bottom right*, p36 *bottom right*, p42 *bottom centre*, p49 *bottom left*, p60 *top*; Jim Newall, p47 *centre*; NHPA, p5 *bottom*, p12 *bottom centre* (G. I. Bernard), p17 *bottom* (Stephen Dalton), p19 *top left* (E. A. Janes), p30 *top right* (Nigel J. Dennis), p35 *bottom left* (Alan Williams), p40 *centre left* (Yves Lanceau), p41 *top left* (John Buckingham), p41 *bottom* (Jonathan & Angela Scott), p44 *top right* (ANT), p48 *bottom left* (Andrew Ackerley), p52 *bottom right* (Rod Planck), p64 *top* (Stephen Dalton), p126 *bottom right* (Dr Ivan Polunien); Oxford Scientific Films, p17 *above centre right* (Sean Morris), p17 *centre left*, (Babs & Bert Wells), p26 *right* (Jim Frazier/Mantis Wildlife Films), p30 *bottom* (Dr C. E. Jeffree), p31 *centre* (J. A. L. Cooke), p31 *bottom* (Michael Fogden), p33 *top right*, p34 *top left*, p34 *bottom centre* (G. I. Bernard), p36 *bottom left* and p39 *centre*, p44 *top centre* (Michael Powles), p37 *centre right* (Mark Hamblin), p38 *top* (Rafi Ben-Shahar), p38 *bottom* (Ian West), p43 *bottom* (Richard Packwood), p54 *top*: tapeworm (James Robinson), p54 *top*: sponge (Konrad Wothe), p68 *top* (Paul Franklin), p75 *bottom right* (NASA), p78 *bottom* (Max Gibbs), p79 *bottom* (Gerard Soury), p32 *top right* (Richard Herrmann), p45 *right* (Ian West), p49 *bottom*; Oxford Scientific Films/London Scientific Films, p12 *top right*, p12 *bottom left*; Panos Pictures/Jean-Leo Dugast, p92; Papilio/Brian Cushing, p19 *bottom*; Pictor, p131 *top*, p138; Popperfoto/Reuters/Mark Baker, p77 *centre*; Renault UK Ltd, p104 *bottom left*, p104 *bottom right*; Rex Features, p99, p113 *left*; Science & Society Picture Library, p76 *bottom*; Science Photo Library, p5 *top*; p8 *centre* (Dr Jeremy Burgess), p12 *top centre*; p12 *bottom right* (Sinclair Stammers), p13 (Moredun Animal Health Ltd), p14 *left* and p21 (Eye of Science), p24 *bottom* (Richard Rawlins/Custom Medical Stock Photo), p26 *left* (Petit Format/Nestle), p26 *centre* (Garry Watson), p32 *bottom right* (William Ervin), p38 *centre right* (Pascal Goetgheluck), p40 *bottom* (Astrid & Hanns-Frieder Michler), p40 *bottom* (Claude Nuridsany & Marie Perennou), p52 *top right* (George Bernard), p52 *centre*; p54 *top*: X-ray of crab (Dave Roberts), p71 *top right* (Dr Jeremy Burgess), p75 *top* (Jerome Yeats), p81 *top left*, p81 *top centre* and p81 *top right* (Martyn F. Chillmaid), p90 *top* (Simon Fraser), p103 *left* (Charles D. Winters), p106 *bottom left* (Tony Craddock), p106 *bottom right* (Craig Miller), p109 *top* (Martin Bond), p109 *centre* (Sheila Terry), p130 *top*, p142 *top* (NASA), p143 *bottom* (J. Pasachoff), p145 (Tom Van Sant/Geosphere Project/Planetary Visions), p148 *bottom*; p149 *bottom* (NASA), p150 (Pekka Parviainen), p151 *left* (Jerry Schad), p151 *centre* (US Naval Observatory); Shout Pictures/John Cullan, p76 *centre*, p77 *bottom left*, p77 *bottom centre*, p77 *bottom right*; Solar Solutions LLC, p95 *left*; Frank Spooner Pictures/GAMMA, p112; Rob Talbot, p69 *top*; Studio Hugo Van Wadenoyen, p47 *above centre right*; Simon Watts, p72 *top*; Wellcome Trust Medical Photographic Library, p20 and p22 (Yorgos Nikas), p42 *bottom left*, p49 *centre*.

Cover photographs by Bill Ivy (Monarch butterfly emerging from cocoon); Getty Images/G. Brad Lewis (Hawaii volcano – lava & cinder cone); Getty Images/Joseph Drivas (Space shuttle after blast-off); Science Photo Library/PLI (Satelite View of Earth).

Project management: Jim Newall
Picture research: Val Mulcahy